Contents

1. Setting the Scene: An Introduction
2. The Historical Context of Early Maps
   - 2.1. Maps Before the Age of Discovery 5
   - 2.2. The Role of Cartography in Exploration 7
   - 2.3. Political and Cultural Impact 10
   - 2.4. Technological Advancements 12
   - 2.5. Influence of Ancient Civilizations 15
3. **The Ottoman Empire and Its Quest for Knowledge** 18
   - 3.1. The Renaissance of Knowledge 18
   - 3.2. Naval Power and Sea Exploration 20
   - 3.3. Piri Reis: The Man Behind the Map 23
   - 3.4. The Court of Selim I 26
   - 3.5. Knowledge Networks of the Era 28
4. **Unfolding the Piri Reis Map** 32
   - 4.1. Discovering the Map 32
   - 4.2. Intricate Details and Annotations 34
   - 4.3. Artistic Influences 35
   - 4.4. Comparisons with Contemporary Maps 38
   - 4.5. Mythical and Allegorical Elements 40
5. **Mapping the Known and the Unknown** 43
   - 5.1. Depictions of Africa 43
   - 5.2. The Enigma of Antarctica 45
   - 5.3. South America's Representation 48
   - 5.4. Imaginary Geographies 50
   - 5.5. Omissions and Alterations 53
6. **The Cartographer's Craft: Techniques and Tools** 56
   - 6.1. Compass, Quadrant, and Astrolabe 56
   - 6.2. The Role of Scaling and Projections 58
   - 6.3. Materials: From Parchment to Ink 60
   - 6.4. Navigational Observations 62
   - 6.5. Evolution of Geographical Thought 65
7. **Perspectives on the New World** 68
   - 7.1. The Old World's Knowledge 68
   - 7.2. The Iberian Influence 70
   - 7.3. The Clash of Old and New Geographies 72
   - 7.4. Cultural Exchange and Expansionism 74
   - 7.5. Legacy of Transformation 76

8. The Art and Science of Cartography 79
   8.1. Blending Art with Science 79
   8.2. Symbols, Legends, and Scales 81
   8.3. Geographical Myths and Realities 83
   8.4. The Aesthetic Appeal of Maps 85
   8.5. Developments into the Modern Era 87

9. Encountering the Map: Reactions and Theories 90
   9.1. Initial Reactions from Historians 90
   9.2. Theories and Hypotheses 92
   9.3. Modern Interpretations 94
   9.4. Challenges to Established History 96
   9.5. The Importance of Re-evaluation 98

10. The Legacy of Piri Reis 101
   10.1. A Lasting Influence on Cartography 101
   10.2. Roles and Perceptions Over Time 103
   10.3. Piri Reis in Popular Culture 105
   10.4. Modern Scholarly Work 107
   10.5. Preservation of the Map 110

The greatest historical works make us realize not just where we came from, but how far we can go.

— Alfred North Whitehead

1. Setting the Scene: An Introduction to the Piri Reis Map

Nestled in the rich tapestry of history, the mysterious Piri Reis Map continues to captivate historians, geographers, and amateur sleuths alike. This relic from the early 16th century offers more than just a glance at the world as it was known half a millennium ago; it challenges our perceptions of history and discovery. Unlike most artifacts that become dust-covered memories of what once was, the Piri Reis Map pulsates with questions, enigmas, and the indelible mark of human curiosity. In this book, we delve into the map's origins, the circumstances of its creation, and the remarkable details that have led to its enduring intrigue. Consider this your guide to exploring one of history's most fascinating cartographical achievements, as we embark on a journey that not only broadens our understanding of the past but expands the horizons of what was thought possible. Join us as we unravel the mysteries and marvels of the Piri Reis Map, a true testament to the spirit of exploration and knowledge.

2. The Historical Context of Early Maps

2.1. Maps Before the Age of Discovery

The history of mapping pre-dates the Age of Discovery by millennia, serving as a testament to humanity's ongoing quest to understand and interpret the surrounding world. Before the spark of exploration that ignited the Age of Discovery in the late 15th century, earlier civilizations laid the foundations of cartography with their rudimentary depictions of geography, showcasing a mixture of knowledge, mythology, and cultural nuance. The journey of these early maps, though often overshadowed by the grand revelations of the explorers who followed, reveals the rich tapestry of human inquiry and its evolution.

In ancient times, maps were not just representations of land; they were artifacts imbued with significance. Civilizations such as the Babylonians, Egyptians, Greeks, and Romans contributed significantly to cartographic tradition. The earliest known map, the Babylonian World Map, or Imago Mundi, from the 6th century BCE, illustrated not only a geographical representation but also offered insights into the cultures that created it. This early cartography was often symbolic, with landscapes demarcated in ways that spoke to the mythology and cosmology of the society it represented, emphasizing the cultural narratives that accompanied the physical world.

The Greeks, particularly figures like Anaximander and Ptolemy, revolutionized mapping by introducing more systematic approaches toward geographic representation. Anaximander is credited with creating one of the first maps of the known world that depicted geographical accuracy relative to the surrounding seas. Ptolemy's work, "Geographia," further refined the techniques of mapping through the introduction of a coordinate system and a comprehensive list of place names, setting a standard for centuries. Ptolemy's maps served as guides that not only directed travelers but also framed an understanding of the world characterized by its known territories and the allure of the unknown.

Roman contributions to cartography were equally significant, benefiting from both administrative needs and military campaigns. The Roman Empire's vast network of roads required precise mapping for logistics and governance. The Tabula Rogeriana, created by the Arab geographer Muhammad al-Idrisi in the 12th century, would synthesize earlier knowledge, drawing on Ptolemaic concepts but incorporating both European and Middle Eastern perspectives. Maps began to reflect societal hierarchies, trade routes, and even the explorers' tales, blending empirical knowledge with speculative features that hinted towards lands yet to be seen.

The medieval period, often deemed the "Dark Ages" for European progress, saw a stagnation in cartographic innovation, but it simultaneously laid the groundwork for a revival in geographic understanding. Maps from this era often merged religious significance with geography. The mappa mundi, for instance, depicted the world in a circular format centered around Jerusalem, reflecting theological perspectives rather than geographic precision. Such maps served not merely as navigational aids but as tools of worldview and morality, marrying earthly geography with celestial oversight.

Islamic scholarship further enriched the cartographic tradition throughout the medieval period, expanding the geographical horizon and introducing the use of detailed maps that depicted intricate trade routes across deserts, seas, and mountain ranges. Scholars like Al-Masudi and Ibn Hawqal compiled maps that were instrumental in enhancing the understanding of the known world, educating their contemporaries on geography that included previously uncharted areas of Asia and Africa.

By the late 15th century, these accumulated practices and knowledge converged, setting the stage for the transformative Age of Discovery. As European explorers sought new trade routes and territories, the existing maps became essential navigational tools, but they also required revision and improvement to encompass the ephemeral nature of newly discovered lands. Innovations in shipbuilding, navigational tools such as the compass and astrolabe, and the increasing desire for accurate representation led to a shift toward a more scientific approach in cartography during this period.

In essence, the maps preceding the Age of Discovery embody a complex interplay of exploration, culture, mythology, and science. They reflect the civilizations' worldviews, aspirations, and understandings, highlighting both the limitations and ambitions of their creators. These early maps laid the groundwork for the Piri Reis Map, propelling humanity from the fringes of the known world into the broader expanses that lay just beyond the horizon—foreshadowing the profound discoveries and cultural exchanges that would unfold in the centuries to come. These pioneering efforts remind us that exploration did not begin with discovery, but rather with an unquenchable curiosity that sought to render the cosmos comprehensible—even if only through sketches, symbols, and an artistic leap toward understanding the infinite complexities of our universe.

2.2. The Role of Cartography in Exploration

The practice of cartography has played a central role in exploration, evolving as an essential tool that not only guided navigators through uncharted waters but also influenced the political, cultural, and economic dynamics of entire civilizations. In the midst of the Age of Discovery, the art and science of map-making transformed significantly, reflecting humanity's profound aspirations to understand, document, and eventually conquer the unknown. Maps served not merely as navigational aids, but as embodiments of knowledge, power, and perspective.

At the heart of exploration lies the necessity for direction and orientation. As explorers braved the vast seas, maps became their stalwart companions. They laid out paths to be followed and territories to be claimed, often derived from a combination of firsthand observations, existing knowledge, and imaginative projections of lands yet to be explored. The Piri Reis Map represents a quintessential example of this dynamic interplay; it not only charted familiar territories but also intertwined these with the speculative, invoking the spirit of both reality and myth. Through this unique blend, the map bridged the known and the unknown, offering explorers both guidance and inspiration.

The accuracy of maps directly influenced navigational techniques. In the absence of modern technology, early explorers relied heavily on celestial navigation, utilizing the stars and the sun's location to orient their journey. With the advancement of cartography, the precision of maps improved, allowing for better understanding of latitudes and longitudes. The developments of navigational instruments, such as the compass and astrolabe, revolutionized the ability to traverse great distances with greater certainty, but these tools were intricately tied to the quality of existing maps. The dual progression of cartographic expertise and technological innovation laid the foundations for safe and successful sea voyages, effectively changing the course of history.

As seafaring expanded, so too did the quest for not only territorial acquisition but also economic advantage. Maps became instruments of imperial ambition, utilized as propaganda to promote the grandeur of a nation's achievements while justifying the expansion of empires. The Piri Reis Map, for instance, served a dual purpose; it was a tool for navigation while also functioning to assert Ottoman power in the Mediterranean and beyond. It underscored the Empire's intellectual endeavors and maritime prowess, elevating its status on the world stage. The implications of cartography thus extended beyond mere representation; they actively shaped the geopolitical landscape as nations vied for control over trade routes and resources.

Furthermore, the artistic dimension of map-making cannot be overlooked. During the Renaissance, maps evolved into spectacular works of art, meticulously embellished and often adorned with intricate illustrations that reflect the imagination of the cartographers. The Piri Reis Map showcases this artistic flair, combining cartographic accuracy with creative depictions of its time. Such maps were not only means of navigation but also statements of cultural identity and aspirations, revealing much about the beliefs, values, and ambitions of the societies that produced them. They illustrated landscapes not only as they were, but as they were envisioned by their creators—layered with mythological references and symbolic allusions that transcended mere geography.

The role of cartography in exploration also encompassed the challenge of depicting and interpreting vast expanses. As explorers encountered lands previously unknown to them, the urgency to record and communicate these discoveries spurred innovations in map-making. While expeditions expanded geographical knowledge, the representations themselves sometimes led to misinterpretations, resulting in mythical lands and creatures populating the maps—an early reflection of how exploratory narratives shaped perceptions of the world. Such embellishments not only highlighted the limitations of knowledge at the time but also revealed the allure of the unknown that fueled human curiosity and ambition.

In examining the rich tapestry of cartography during the era of exploration, one must acknowledge the collaborative spirit among cultures. The transfer of knowledge across civilizations played a pivotal role in shaping maps. The Piri Reis Map, for instance, embodies a synthesis of information accumulated from various sources, including European maritime charts, indigenous knowledge, and earlier Ottoman navigational maps. This intermingling of knowledge showcases how cartography became a medium for cultural exchange, illustrating the interconnectedness of diverse explorative endeavors.

Ultimately, the significance of cartography in exploration transcends its utility as a tool. It reflects a vital dialogue between discovery and representation, knowledge and power, art and science. Cartographers and explorers operated as pioneers, pushing boundaries and expanding horizons while transforming human understanding of the world. The maps of the past, including the remarkable Piri Reis Map, serve as timeless artifacts that encapsulate the spirit of exploration, standing as testaments to humanity's ceaseless quest for knowledge and discovery. As we continue to unravel the mysteries encoded in such maps, we honor the legacy of those who dared to explore and document the unknown—a legacy that resonates through the pages of history and continues to inspire future generations.

2.3. Political and Cultural Impact

The Piri Reis Map functions not merely as a navigational tool but as a captivating artifact to examine the intertwining forces of political power and cultural exchange during the early 16th century. Maps, throughout history, have served multiple roles—depicting geographical boundaries, defining imperial ambitions, and shaping national identities. They are reflections of not just the landscapes they portray, but also the societies, political systems, and cultural narratives that produce them.

As the Ottoman Empire emerged as a significant force during the late medieval period, it harnessed the power of cartography to symbolize its political might. The Piri Reis Map, crafted during the reign of Sultan Selim I, is emblematic of this phenomenon. With it, Piri Reis not only charted the known world but also articulated the aspirations of an empire that sought to extend its influence over vast territories. In the empire's quest to assert control over the Mediterranean and the trade routes that interlinked Europe, Asia, and Africa, the map became an instrument of statecraft, showcasing the empire's reach and asserting its dominance over maritime affairs.

This political utility of maps is underscored by how they served to project power both internally and externally. Internally, maps functioned as tools to stabilize and govern vast territories, providing an authoritative representation of the empire's dominions. They informed policies regarding resource allocation, military mobilizations, and trade activities, creating a sense of order and coherence in a sprawling political entity. Externally, maps acted as declarations of intent, laying claim to territories both known and unknown, molding perceptions of an empire's capabilities. The presentation of territories on maps influenced diplomatic relations and was often used to justify territorial claims in negotiations with other powers.

Culturally, the Piri Reis Map encapsulates a confluence of knowledge systems and cultural exchanges that transcended geographical boundaries. As a product of an era characterized by significant intercultural interaction, the map reflects the synthesis of various navigational methodologies and geographic knowledge amassed from diverse cultures. The collaboration between Greek, Arab, and European texts infused cartography with a rich tapestry of information that could be leveraged in different contexts. This exchange of knowledge was particularly pronounced during the Age of Discovery, as explorers interacted with indigenous populations, assimilating their insights and reflecting them on maps.

The artistic elements found within the Piri Reis Map reveal the cultural nuances of the time. The vibrant colors, intricate illustrations, and detailed annotations serve not only to document geographical features but also to tell the stories of the peoples that inhabited these lands. Such rich depictions illustrate daily life, trade, and encounters between different cultures, forming a narrative that extends beyond mere geography. This artistic interpretation of geography reflects the Ottoman Empire's engagement with the world. It showcases an appreciation of cultures, underscoring a cultural narrative that acknowledges the interconnectedness of humans and places across the globe.

The political and cultural impact of the Piri Reis Map is compounded by its historical position at a juncture of expanding geographic knowledge and increasing imperial ambition. As European powers embarked on their exploratory ventures, the Piri Reis Map was situated amidst this global transformation in understanding both land and maritime domains. It symbolized the Ottoman Empire's intellectual pride, conveying the idea that it was not just a military power but also a center of knowledge and learning capable of engaging with the complexities of global navigation.

Furthermore, the Piri Reis Map laid the groundwork for future cartographic endeavors by influencing subsequent map-making practices. The political narrative inherent in its creation persisted, as emerging powers recognized the importance of mapping as a means of asserting authority and expressing cultural identity. The map exemplified how the act of cartography was, in essence, a reflection of power relations as well as a vehicle for promoting cultural narratives, fostering trading partnerships, and legitimizing territorial claims—each of which resonated throughout the ages to influence the course of world history.

Ultimately, the Piri Reis Map serves as a remarkable testament to the deep connections between cartography, culture, and power during its time. It stands not just as a geographical representation but as an enduring symbol of a multifaceted dynamic, encompassing the desires, fears, and ambitions of its creators and their societies. As we reflect on the map's legacy, it becomes clear that it is an artifact through which we can explore broader themes of human expression and connection—narratives that continue to evolve and resonate in our understanding of the world today.

2.4. Technological Advancements

The exploration of technological advancements during the early 16th century illuminates how innovations shaped cartographic practices, ultimately culminating in the creation of remarkable maps such as the Piri Reis Map. This period, characterized by a confluence of practical needs, scientific curiosity, and artistic pursuits, saw significant progress in navigation, mapmaking methodologies, and tools. These advancements would provide the framework that allowed Piri Reis and his contemporaries to not only document the existing world but to challenge and expand the boundaries of the known.

At the heart of these technological advancements lies the evolution of navigational instruments that transformed seafaring and cartography. Prior to the 16th century, navigators relied heavily on celestial bodies, such as stars and the sun, to ascertain their positions at sea. However, the development of the compass in the late medieval period provided a reliable means for sailors to maintain a consistent direction regardless of geographic or environmental challenges. This simple yet revolutionary device allowed explorers to venture deeper into uncharted waters with increased confidence.

The astrolabe, another pivotal navigational advancement, became essential for determining latitude by measuring the angle of celestial bodies above the horizon. Invented in ancient times but refined during the Middle Ages, the astrolabe was crucial for celestial navigation. Sailors could plot their positions and adjust their courses according to the readings, thus enabling longer oceanic voyages. The combination of the compass and astrolabe not only enhanced the technical capabilities of navigators but also empowered cartographers to create more accurate representations of the Earth.

Simultaneously, advances in shipbuilding techniques played a vital role in enhancing exploration capabilities. The introduction of the caravel—a small, highly maneuverable ship—during the Age of Discovery exemplified the fusion of various shipbuilding traditions from different cultures. The caravel allowed for better sails and hull designs that could safely navigate rough waters and endure long journeys. Combined with updated navigational tools, these ships opened up the seas, allowing explorers to chart new territories and collect geographical data that would be documented in maps.

Cartography itself underwent a transformative journey during this epoch, transitioning from symbolic interpretations of the world into a more scientific endeavor. The integration of mathematics and geometry into map-making facilitated the precise scaling and projection of geographical features onto flat surfaces. Notable cartographers started employing methods such as triangulation and the use of grid systems. This informed the creation of more reliable map projections, making it possible to depict the curvature of the Earth in a two-dimensional format. Piri Reis's map, influenced by these techniques, would illustrate both known regions and speculative uncharted territories, merging empirical observation with theoretical understanding.

Another significant technological advancement was the introduction of printing techniques. The advent of movable type printing in the mid-15th century revolutionized the spread of geographic knowledge. Published maps could now reach a wider audience, enhancing literacy rates and fostering a greater public interest in navigation and discovery. This increased accessibility allowed explorers, publishers, and universities alike to disseminate knowledge that had previously been confined to manuscript formats. The mass production of maps ensured that explorers would embark with the freshest knowledge available—exemplified through updating existing maps with new findings, like those represented in the Piri Reis Map.

Alongside these advancements, the standards of map accuracy underwent scrutiny and improvements. The intersection of various knowledge networks—trading posts, academic institutions, and exploration accounts—yielded rich insight into the collection of data from both European and indigenous sources. The cross-pollination of knowledge enabled cartographers to enrich their maps with firsthand observations, cultural narratives, and commercial insights, leading to a broader understanding of both familiar and foreign spaces. Piri Reis, as a member of the Ottoman naval tradition, exemplified this ethos, borrowing from rich traditions while contributing original observations from Ottoman explorations in the Mediterranean and beyond.

The cartographic techniques employed during this age also involved artistic elements, blending scientific expediency with aesthetic considerations. Maps began to include intricate visual elements—ornamental borders, illustrations of sea monsters, compass roses, and elaborate depictions of flora and fauna that featured in different regions. These embellishments served not only to engage viewers but also to communicate cultural narratives interwoven within geographical data. The artistic style found in the Piri Reis Map not only elevates it as a functional guide but also as a piece of cultural expression reflective of its time.

The technological advancements of the 16th century, therefore, laid fertile ground for the creation of the Piri Reis Map, opening the door to a new understanding of the world. The convergence of improved navigational tools, enhanced ship design, rigorous mathematical practices, and the transformative power of print catalyzed a shift in how humanity perceived and interacted with its environment. The intricate tapestry of map-making during this era served as much more than a collection of directions; it embodied human ambition, curiosity, and the relentless quest to decipher the unknown. As we study the legacy of the Piri Reis Map, we recognize it not just as an artifact of its time but as a landmark realization of technological enterprise in cartography—an endeavor that continues to inspire modern exploration and geographical interpretation.

2.5. Influence of Ancient Civilizations

In tracing the lineage of cartographic traditions that influenced later map-making practices, one cannot overlook the profound impact of ancient civilizations such as the Greeks, Romans, and even earlier cultures. The evolution of cartography is marked by a continuity of ideas, methods, and cultural exchanges that paved the way for remarkable achievements, including the Piri Reis Map. By delving deep into these influences, we gain a rich understanding of how historical contexts and intellectual advancements reshaped human knowledge of the world, ultimately leading to the creation of maps that redefined navigation and exploration.

Greek contributions to cartography were foundational, establishing principles and methodologies that would resonate through the centuries. In the 6th century BCE, Anaximander constructed one of the earliest known maps, which portrayed the world in a way that sought not only geographical accuracy but also philosophical contemplation of existence. His map depicted a flat Earth and introduced the concept of mapping territories based on observation rather than mere speculation. Ptolemy later revolutionized Greek cartography with his seminal text, "Geographia," published in the 2nd century CE. In this work, Ptolemy introduced a coordinate system of latitude and longitude that allowed for unprecedented precision in mapping. His utilization of systematic observations and a database of place names became a standard practice, influencing medieval and later European mapmakers.

However, it was the Roman Empire that extended and institutionalized these Greek ideas, applying them to suit the needs of a vast imperial network. Roman maps, like the Tabula Rogeriana and the Peutinger Table, showcased not only geographical features but also facilitated military and trade logistics across the empire. The Romans' emphasis on infrastructure, roads, and navigable rivers highlighted their practical approach to cartography. This blend of Greek philosophical insight and Roman empirical needs laid the groundwork for future advancements in map-making, inspiring cartographers to merge artistry with scientific inquiry.

The fusion of knowledge did not stop with the fall of the Western Roman Empire. Ancient cartography saw significant re-engagement, particularly through Islamic scholarship during the medieval period. Islamic scholars preserved and translated Greek and Roman texts, further advancing cartographic knowledge. Figures like Al-Ma'mun and Al-Idrisi contributed detailed geographic works that synthesized earlier traditions with observations from explorations across the Arab world, Africa, and parts of Asia. This period marked a resurgence in geographic curiosity, with maps evolving in complexity, decoration, and accuracy. Islamic cartographers often included intricate illustrations that depicted topographical features alongside cultural elements, reflecting the dynamic interplay of trade, culture, and navigation.

The achievements of ancient civilizations culminated in a dialogue of knowledge that set the stage for the Renaissance's revival of classical thought. With the advent of the Age of Discovery in the late 15th century, explorers were equipped with the accumulated wisdom of centuries. As Europeans sought new territories, their maps drew from ancient cartographic traditions, severing the long-held notions of a flat Earth depicted in early medieval maps. Instead, they ventured into a three-dimensional understanding of the world, merging the scientific principles introduced by the Greeks and refined by the Romans with the rich cultural observations offered by Islamic scholars.

The influence of these ancient civilizations is strikingly apparent in the methodologies employed by cartographers like Piri Reis. His map is a product of both empirical observation and cultural synthesis, reflecting the extensive geographic knowledge accumulated from prior traditions. Piri Reis's combination of European nautical charts, Arabic navigational wisdom, and indigenous knowledge encapsulates this vibrant legacy, illustrating how ancient practices persistently informed and enhanced the craft of cartography.

Moreover, the artistic dimensions of ancient map-making carried over into the 16th century, evidenced by Piri Reis's vivid depictions and embellishments. Mapmakers continued to embrace the aesthetically engaging styles of the past, blending geographical representation with mythical creatures and grand narratives. This artistic tradition not only enriched the maps themselves but also invoked a cultural dialogue that celebrated exploration as a vital facet of human experience.

The remarkable continuity of cartographic practice, from ancient Greece and Rome through to the Islamic Golden Age and into the Renaissance, ultimately shaped the way the world was navigated and understood. The Piri Reis Map stands as a testament to this trajectory, encapsulating centuries of knowledge and cultural exchange that facilitated exploration. As we consider the profound influence of ancient civilizations on subsequent map-making, we recognize that every line drawn on these maps is not merely geographic representation but a reflection of human endeavor, creativity, and the insatiable quest to understand and define our place in the world. It is this enduring legacy of inquiry—rooted in the ancient past—that informs our modern interpretations and aspirations in the realm of mapping and exploration.

3. The Ottoman Empire and Its Quest for Knowledge

3.1. The Renaissance of Knowledge

The Ottoman Empire, during its zenith in the early 16th century, found itself at a unique crossroads of history—a point where a confluence of ancient knowledge and emergent scientific inquiry created fertile ground for intellectual growth. This period, commonly referred to as the Renaissance of Knowledge, marked a revival in curiosity across various domains such as astronomy, geography, mathematics, and philosophy, rekindled through the synthesis of knowledge from different civilizations. The Piri Reis Map, originating from this milieu, embodies the embodiment of this spirit of exploration and learning.

As the Ottoman Empire expanded its borders and influence, it inadvertently became a melting pot of cultures, ideas, and information. The Empire's strategic location, straddling Europe and Asia, positioned it as a critical conduit for the transmission of knowledge. Scholars, traders, and diplomats often interacted within this expansive territory, sharing insights and experiences from distant lands. This exchange was not merely incidental; it reflected deliberate policies by the Sultans, particularly under the rule of Selim I, who sought to bolster the Empire's intellectual and cultural status. Historians often note that this openness to various streams of knowledge, including the revival of Greco-Roman texts through Islamic scholarship, laid a rich intellectual groundwork that Piri Reis would leverage in his cartographic practice.

The pursuit of knowledge during this era was increasingly rigorous and methodical. The Ottoman Empire itself developed educational institutions—madrasas—that were dedicated to studying various disciplines, including astronomy and geography. Here, scholars compiled and translated texts, creating an environment laden with intellectual fervor. This foundation paved the way for contributions to cartography, as practitioners like Piri Reis undertook extensive studies, gathering data from multiple sources. The Empire gravitated towards collecting navigational knowledge; maritime exploration became an area of great interest as it not only extended trade routes but also strengthened military power.

Piri Reis himself represents an amalgamation of this era's intellectual pursuits. As a naval officer and cartographer, he translated and synthesized a wealth of information from earlier maps and texts along with firsthand observations from his voyages across the Mediterranean and beyond. The Piri Reis Map serves as a vivid testament to his endeavors, reflecting an array of civilizations—European, African, and Asian influences, intertwined through a framework established by ancient scholars and revived by contemporary thought.

Moreover, during this period, the concept of scientific inquiry began to take a more empirical form. Maps were being refined not just as artistic representations of the world, but as meticulous documents grounded in observations and measurements. The use of navigational instruments like the astrolabe and quadrant became standard practice, seeking veracity in latitude and longitude that had once been speculative. Piri Reis's cartographic practices were informed by this new spirit; his work emerged from an understanding that maps could convey not just territory but also knowledge crafted through systematic observation.

However, the Renaissance of Knowledge extended beyond mere nautical navigation; it encompassed a broader outlook on science and philosophy. The introduction of new ideas, such as heliocentrism and advancements in the natural sciences, also influenced Ottoman thought. Scholars began to question long-held beliefs, seeking greater accuracy and understanding of the cosmos and the geographical sphere. The interaction between this intellectual awakening and the Ottoman lattice of cultures propelled explorers further into uncharted territories, with maps increasingly used as platforms for asserting knowledge and power on a global scale.

The extension of maritime exploration coincided with territorial expansions, driven not only by economic interests but also an eagerness to catalog the known world. As the newly-founded empires sought to assert their geopolitical power, understanding and representing these territories became of utmost importance. The Piri Reis Map, with its artistic renderings and careful annotations, embodied this quest—providing not only geographical data but also reflecting the Empire's intellectual engagement with its surroundings.

Furthermore, the sharing of information across borders and disciplines facilitated this expansive quest for knowledge. The Ottoman Empire's diplomatic relations fostered environments where various cultures could exchange ideas freely. The networks of trade that linked Europe with Asia and Africa became channels for the diffusion of knowledge, integrating scientific advancements and empirical understanding across continents. This cross-pollination of ideas was instrumental in shaping Piri Reis's work; the map revealed how the convergence of many strands of inquiry could lead to a holistic understanding of the world.

In conclusion, the Renaissance of Knowledge within the Ottoman Empire did not exist in isolation. It represented a dynamic interplay between curiosity, cultural exchange, and the inexorable quest for mastery over the natural world. The Piri Reis Map emanates from this fertile intellectual landscape as a symbol of the early 16th-century spirit of exploration. It captures not merely a geographical representation but also the essence of an era driven by the relentless pursuit of knowledge, reflecting a time when humanity sought to expand not just the map but the very boundaries of understanding itself. As we examine this pivotal moment in history, we recognize the enduring legacy of Piri Reis and his contemporaries—an inspiration that continues to resonate in today's collective quest for knowledge and discovery.

3.2. Naval Power and Sea Exploration

The ascent of the Ottoman Empire in the early 16th century marked a pivotal moment in naval power and maritime exploration, establishing it as a formidable player on the world stage. This period of expansion was characterized by a remarkable amalgamation of military prowess, innovative maritime technologies, and an insatiable thirst for knowledge. The empire's naval forces emerged not merely as instruments of warfare but as conduits of exploration, commerce, and cultural exchange that fundamentally reshaped the global landscape.

Central to the Ottoman naval endeavor was the strategic vision of its leaders, particularly Sultan Selim I. Under his reign, the empire sought to expand its influence across the Mediterranean and into the Indian Ocean, regions that were pivotal for trade and cultural exchanges. Recognizing the significance of maritime dominance, Selim I invested heavily in the development of the navy, transforming it into an advanced fleet capable of projecting power and safeguarding trade routes. The Ottoman naval power was not just about military supremacy; it was also about the absorption of knowledge from the cultures it encountered, leading to significant contributions to cartography and navigation.

The Ottoman naval forces were equipped with an array of ships, including galleys and later galleons, each designed to optimize speed, maneuverability, and firepower. These vessels became the backbone of naval operations, allowing the empire to assert control over vital waterways. Capturing key maritime cities such as Rhodes and expanding into the Red Sea enabled the Ottomans to establish a formidable network of ports and supply routes, facilitating both military expeditions and trade.

At the confluence of naval power and exploration was the relentless pursuit of knowledge about the seas and the lands beyond them. Ottoman sailors and navigators sought to chart unfamiliar waters, mapping coastlines, islands, and harbors as they ventured into new territories. This spirit of inquiry was exemplified by figures like Piri Reis, whose contributions to cartography illustrated not only the capabilities of the Ottoman navy but also the broader aspirations of the empire.

The Piri Reis Map itself stands as a testament to this age of naval exploration. Compiled in 1513, it is a synthesis of knowledge gathered from a plethora of sources, including earlier maps, explorations, and navigational accounts. Piri Reis's work encapsulated the integration of regional knowledge with broader explorative ambitions, drawing upon Greek, Roman, Arab, and even medieval European influences. It illustrated the significant maritime routes of the time, delineating the Mediterranean and parts of the New World, reflecting the blending of various cultural insights that characterized the Ottoman approach to exploration.

Moreover, maritime exploration during this period was not limited to the pursuit of new territories. The Ottomans actively engaged with indigenous populations and local cultures, enriching their understanding of geography. The knowledge acquired through interactions with diverse maritime communities not only enhanced Piri Reis's cartographic projects but also contributed to the empire's military and economic strategies. An awareness of local trade practices, customs, and environmental conditions fostered relationships that were crucial for sustaining Ottoman hegemony in newly acquired regions.

The advancements in maritime technology during the 16th century significantly complemented the Ottoman naval expansion. The introduction of sophisticated navigational instruments enabled sailors to traverse oceans with greater precision. The astrolabe, quadrant, and later developments in ship design allowed for more accurate mapping of the stars and coastlines. These instruments facilitated the strategic planning of voyages, ensuring that Ottoman sailors could make informed decisions while exploring new waters.

Simultaneously, the advent of printed maps in the Renaissance played a transformative role in disseminating geographic knowledge. The emergence of printing technology allowed for the widespread reproduction of navigational charts and atlases, democratizing access to cartographic knowledge. This influx of information enriched the Ottoman understanding of the world, making it possible for seafarers to guide their vessels with the most accurate representations of the seas and lands they traversed.

The influence of Ottoman naval power extended far beyond mere military might; it established trade networks that connected Europe, Africa, and Asia. The empire became a key player in the spice trade, and its maritime routes facilitated the exchange of not only goods but also cultural and scientific ideas. By controlling access to vital trading routes, the Ottomans ensured their status as a dominant economic force, which in turn fueled further exploration and cartographic endeavors.

In conclusion, the Ottoman Empire's rise in naval power during the 16th century was a multifaceted phenomenon encompassing military expansion, technological advancements, and a profound commitment to exploration. The empire's naval forces not only asserted dominance across critical maritime pathways but also served as vehicles of knowledge, enabling the exchange of ideas and cultural practices. Piri Reis's creation of his famous map reflects this rich tapestry of naval craftsmanship and intellectual curiosity, standing as a meaningful artifact that illustrates the empire's broader mission to explore, document, and understand the world. In unraveling the narrative of Ottoman maritime exploration, we come to appreciate the lasting impact of this era—one that would shape global interactions and cartographic practices well into the future.

3.3. Piri Reis: The Man Behind the Map

Piri Reis emerged from a confluence of historical currents that defined the early 16th century—a period marked by fervent exploration and the quest for knowledge. Born in 1465 in present-day Turkey, he played a pivotal role in shaping the maritime landscape of the Ottoman Empire. His life encapsulated the myriad forces at play during an era of profound change, where the boundaries of the known world were continuously being redrawn, and the thirst for geographical knowledge was reaching unprecedented heights.

As a member of the Ottoman naval tradition, Piri Reis was deeply influenced by the maritime culture permeating through the Empire. He began his career in the marine environment early on, drawn to the life of adventure offered by the sea. His early years were likely spent as part of maritime expeditions, providing him with firsthand experiences and insights into navigation, cartography, and the diverse cultures that inhabited the coastal regions of the Mediterranean and beyond. Piri Reis's experiences at sea would ultimately inform his later work and contribute to his reputation as a skilled navigator.

Piri Reis's foundational education in navigation and cartography drew upon a rich array of sources, significantly impacting the way he approached map-making. His knowledge was likely enhanced by the intersection of cultures within the Ottoman Empire, which collected and preserved vast amounts of knowledge from antiquity, particularly from Greek and Arab scholars. The process of translating and synthesizing these diverse geographical texts provided a fertile ground for Piri Reis's own cartographic innovations.

Key to his development as a cartographer was the recognition of the importance of observation and empirical data collection. Unlike many of his contemporaries, who relied heavily on speculative information, Piri Reis took meticulous notes from his voyages. This emphasis on observation allowed him to create maps that not only reflected the geographical realities of his time but also bridged the existing knowledge with new discoveries that came from his exploratory voyages. Such a methodology placed Piri Reis at the forefront of Ottoman maritime navigation and turned him into a prominent figure within the empire.

A significant milestone in Piri Reis's career came in 1513 when he completed his most famous work—the Piri Reis Map. This map is not only a remarkable achievement in cartography but a profoundly meaningful artifact that reveals the interwoven nature of knowledge, culture, and exploration. The creation of the map was likely inspired by the confluence of contemporary knowledge stemming from recent explorations by European powers such as Spain and Portugal, as well as from the navigation records and charts that had come through Islamic scholarship. The Piri Reis Map is notable for its synthesis; it incorporates a diverse array of information that includes not just European maritime maps but also indigenous knowledge passed down through generations. Each segment of the map tells a story—of people, places, and the ceaseless quest for understanding of the world.

The intricacies of the Piri Reis Map reflect both an artistic endeavor and the scientific rigor of his time. The map, adorned with vibrant illustrations, demarcated coastlines, and annotations, conveyed geographical knowledge as well as cultural insights. Piri Reis utilized rich artistic elements to embellish his work, including images of mythical sea creatures and depictions of the landscapes he encountered, transforming the map from a mere navigational guide into a narrative of exploration. This mediated the realities of exploration experienced by Ottoman sailors and offered them a richer context within which to understand their world.

Piri Reis's status as an influential figure went beyond pure navigation and cartography. He stood at the helm of an Ottoman naval renaissance, tasked with expanding the empire's maritime dominance. His writings, including the "Kitab-ı Bahriye" (Book of Navigation), further solidified his expertise by offering detailed descriptions of the coasts and maritime routes of the Mediterranean. Through his work, he established a legacy of intellectual engagement and inquiry that resonated throughout the empire and beyond.

Despite his accomplishments, the latter part of Piri Reis's life was marked by the complexities of imperial ambitions and the inherent challenges faced by those who dare to explore new territories. His career reflects the broader societal currents of the time—an age marked by competition among emerging empires and the continuous need for exploration to sustain political power, navigate trade, and secure cultural superiority.

The legacy of Piri Reis can be seen today as a profound intersection of exploration, culture, and science. His contributions to cartography laid the foundations for future mapmakers and influenced the realm of geographical knowledge for generations to come. As historians delve into his story, they uncover not just a cartographer but a symbol of an era that sought to expand the horizons of human knowledge —a period where maps were not only tools for navigation but also vessels of culture, narrative, and ambition. The Piri Reis Map, as an artifact of this legacy, continues to captivate and inspire, serving as a reminder of humanity's enduring quest to understand and map the world around us.

3.4. The Court of Selim I

Within the vibrant cultural and intellectual landscape of the Ottoman Empire during the early 16th century, the court of Sultan Selim I represented a unifying force for scholarly pursuits and explorative ambitions. It was here that Piri Reis created his celebrated map, a product of a dynamic milieu that fused tradition with innovation. Selim I's reign marked a pivotal moment for the empire, not only in military expansion but also in fostering a thirst for knowledge. As the empire expanded its territorial reach, so too did its influence over the exchange of ideas, scientific inquiry, and cultural practices. The environment cultivated within the court of Selim I became fertile ground for intellectual curiosity and ambition.

Selim I, known for his authoritative leadership and strategic military campaigns, recognized the significance of knowledge in consolidating his power. The Ottoman court was not merely a political hub, but also an intellectual assembly that attracted scholars, navigators, and scientists from various corners of the empire and beyond. This cross-cultural interaction facilitated an exchange of ideas that transcended geographic boundaries, encompassing knowledge from the ancient Greeks, Roman cartographic traditions, and Arabic scholarship. The court became a repository of insights drawn from multiple civilizations, an enterprise in which Piri Reis played a central role as a cartographer deeply committed to the synthesis of accumulated wisdom.

In this environment, the ideals of Renaissance humanism began to permeate the Ottoman intellectual ethos. Scholars at the Ottoman court sought to reconcile various strands of knowledge, intricately weaving together classical texts, empirical observations, and local lore. The commission of maps and navigational guides became emblematic of this spirit, as they served as instruments of both exploration and imperial identity. The creation of the Piri Reis Map not only reflects the technical aspects of cartography but also embodies the intellectual currents that swirled around Selim I's court, showcasing a vision of the world that was both expansive and inclusive.

Piri Reis, an embodiment of this milieu, was not only a skilled navigator but also a thinker who synthesized diverse influences into his work. His map exemplified the integration of knowledge gathered from various sources—European nautical charts, Arabic navigational texts, and indigenous accounts. The Ottoman Empire, under Selim I, had a vested interest in maritime trade and exploration. As a result, the production of accurate navigational aids was paramount for maintaining security along the empire's coastal routes and facilitating expansion in newly encountered territories. The court's support for projects like those of Piri Reis illustrated the deliberate connection between knowledge generation and the empire's geopolitical aspirations.

Furthermore, the atmosphere at Selim I's court fostered innovation and artistic expression. Piri Reis's talents were not confined to technical skills; he was also an artist who understood the necessity of embellishment in cartography. The aesthetic elements of the Piri Reis Map—its vivid colors, artistic depictions of fauna and flora, and elaborate borders—reflect broader cultural inclinations towards beauty and detail that were encouraged in the court. The Ottoman emphasis on art as an extension of intellectual inquiry set the stage for maps to become not just tools of navigation but also cultural artifacts that conveyed stories about the empire's reach and ambitions.

Moreover, Selim I's policies promoted the development of knowledge networks that engaged in interdisciplinary collaborations, laying the groundwork for advancements in astronomy, mathematics, medicine, and geography. The establishment of madrasas and libraries within the empire provided scholars with resources and spaces for dialogue, enabling the rise of a sophisticated intellectual community. The Piri Reis Map emerged not just as a product of one individual's labor but as a culmination of collective scholarly endeavors that permeated the court and the broader society.

The map's very creation involved an intricate process of gathering data, crafting representations, and interpreting observations of the world. Piri Reis was conscious of both the technical demands of map-making and the responsibilities it conferred. His work reflected an understanding that the empire's navigators relied on such maps for exploration and trade, solidifying the connection between cartography and imperial identity.

In conclusion, the court of Selim I formed a nexus of knowledge that supported and propelled a wave of intellectual endeavor, engaged in exploration, navigation, and cultural expression. Within this rich tapestry, Piri Reis found the intellectual and artistic backing to produce the Piri Reis Map. The map symbolizes not only a technical achievement in cartography but also a reflection of the dynamic cultural syncretism and intellectual inquiry that characterized Selim I's reign. As we study the environment in which this remarkable artifact was produced, we better appreciate the profound intersections of knowledge, ambition, and artistry that define the Ottoman legacy and the spirit of exploration as captured in the Piri Reis Map.

3.5. Knowledge Networks of the Era

The knowledge networks of the early 16th century formed an intricate tapestry that facilitated the exchange and accumulation of geographical information. These networks were paramount in shaping the era's understanding not only of known territories but also of vast stretches of uncharted lands, ultimately leading to groundbreaking cartographic achievements like the Piri Reis Map. At the heart of these networks lay a variety of channels—trade routes, academic institutions, adventurer accounts, and diplomatic relations

—each contributing to the larger landscape of knowledge that would guide explorers across the world's oceans.

Trade routes served as crucial arteries through which information flowed; they were not merely pathways for goods and commodities but also conduits for ideas and knowledge transfer. Across the Mediterranean, the Silk Road, and the burgeoning Atlantic routes, merchants, sailors, and diplomats encountered diverse cultures, each with its own intellectual contributions. Arab traders, who had long been navigating these routes, were particularly instrumental in this cultural exchange, carrying with them texts and maps derived from earlier civilizations—Greek, Roman, and Persian. This cross-pollination of knowledge introduced new geographic concepts and navigational techniques to European thinkers, who were eager to expand their understanding of the world.

Additionally, the rise of port cities as centers of commerce and scholarship enabled the convergence of diverse intellectual traditions. Cities such as Venice, Genoa, and Istanbul became melting pots of ideas where cartographers, navigators, and scholars could interact and collaborate. These cities not only serviced the demands of trade but also facilitated the growth of libraries and centers of learning where knowledge could be stored, debated, and disseminated. The Piri Reis Map itself was a product of such learning, synthesized from a wealth of sources circulated through these vibrant hubs of commerce and knowledge.

Traveler accounts further enriched this web of knowledge networks. As explorers embarked on voyages into the unknown, their firsthand experiences became valuable sources of information that fed into the cartographic traditions of the time. Accounts of new lands, peoples, and trade opportunities were eagerly shared among scholars, spurring further explorations and engendering a spirit of curiosity. Piri Reis's own maritime adventures across the Mediterranean and beyond enabled him to gather firsthand information, which he translated into his maps. His synthesis of knowledge from both European navigational charts and indigenous accounts of the New World exemplifies this dynamic—even as he drew upon ancient and contemporary sources to inform his own work.

Diplomatic exchanges also played a significant role in facilitating the flow of knowledge. As empires sought to expand their territories and exert influence, diplomatic envoys became carriers of information, passing along insights gleaned from their travels. Letters, treaties, and reports not only charted political landscapes but also conveyed geographic knowledge, illuminating the complexities of lands beyond familiar territories. Ottoman diplomatic missions interacted with European powers and engaged in negotiations that often turned scholarly. The intellectual curiosity fostered by these relationships further propelled cartographic advances as newly acquired knowledge was incorporated into maps.

A crucial element within these knowledge networks was the ongoing communication among scholars. The rise of universities and madrasas during this period promoted educational efforts that encompassed geography and navigation. Scholars collected and annotated earlier texts, preserving ancient knowledge while integrating new discoveries. Works by scientists like Al-Idrisi were critical; his geographical treatise drew from numerous existing sources, creating a compendium of information that would influence subsequent generations of cartographers. The accumulation of intelligence through scholarly exchanges laid the groundwork for significant improvements in cartography—improvements seen in the meticulous detailing of maps like that of Piri Reis.

Furthermore, the Renaissance's emphasis on empiricism and observation marked a turning point in how knowledge was approached. This shift in thought encouraged explorers and mapmakers alike to prioritize hands-on experience and rigorous documentation of findings. Scholars began to understand the necessity of accurate representations in mapping, which aligned perfectly with the ambitions of empires vying for power and resources. The marriage of empirical observation with traditional knowledge resulted in a more nuanced and complete understanding of the world, influencing how maps were rendered and interpreted.

Thus, the knowledge networks of the 16th century can be seen as a complex interplay of trade, scholarship, exploration, and diplomacy. Each channel contributed to a robust exchange of ideas, fostering a spirit of inquiry that extended beyond mere navigation into the realms of culture, science, and identity. The Piri Reis Map stands as a prime example of this dynamic, illustrating how the confluence of diverse knowledge streams constructed a richer cartographic narrative. The legacies of these networks would resonate for generations, shaping not only the era's explorations but also the very understanding of geography itself. As history continues to unfold, these intricate connections highlight the ever-relevant importance of collaboration and the sharing of knowledge in the pursuit of discovery.

4. Unfolding the Piri Reis Map

4.1. Discovering the Map

The thrilling discovery of the Piri Reis Map in the dusty annals of the Topkapi Palace is a captivating story that intertwines history, intrigue, and the enduring quest for knowledge. The map, one of the most significant cartographic achievements of the early 16th century, was not just a relic; it was a key that opened the door to a multitude of questions about the nature of exploration, the extent of geographic knowledge, and the cultures that shaped its creation.

The Piri Reis Map was rediscovered in 1929, tucked away within a stack of historical documents that had gathered dust in the Ottoman Empire's most prestigious museum. The Topkapi Palace, a symbol of imperial power, housed countless artifacts from the glorious past of the Ottomans, and among these treasures, the map lay in wait for a momentous revelation. This marked an exciting moment in the realm of historical cartography, as scholars recognized that this exquisite piece of parchment held the key to understanding the complex network of exploration and knowledge exchange in the early modern world.

Its initial unveiling provided a stark contrast to the conventional depictions of the known world at the time. Scholars and historians alike stared in awe at the intricate drawings that encompassed vast territories spanning from Europe to Asia, and even parts of the New World, which had only recently come to the attention of European navigators. The map's detailed annotations and artistic embellishments, including images of monsters and mythological creatures, further highlighted the vibrant culture from which it emerged, intertwining scientific inquiry with artistic expression.

The event of the map's discovery set into motion a wave of scholarly interest, leading historians to explore the cartographic techniques employed by Piri Reis. As experts scrutinized the map, they unearthed connections to the cultural currents of the era, reflecting the rich interplay between European explorers, Ottoman scholars, and indigenous knowledge. The map was not merely a static representation of geographical features; it was a document imbued with the aspirations and narratives of multiple cultures, a testament to the spirit of exploration that characterized this period.

Piri Reis's work resonated deeply within the context of the Age of Discovery, as it encapsulated the convergence of knowledge from various sources, including earlier maps and ancient texts. The map illustrated Piri Reis's ingenious ability to blend empirical observations from his voyages with existing cartographic knowledge, creating a rich tapestry of geography that showcased the breadth of exploration undertaken by the Ottomans and their contemporaries.

As the broader implications of the Piri Reis Map began to surface, it catalyzed discussions around the challenges faced by early cartographers in their quest to accurately depict the world. The inaccuracies that surfaced—from speculative landmasses to mythical representations of creatures in the seas—fueled debates about the nature of knowledge and the limitations of contemporary understanding. The map exemplified both the triumphs and the tribulations of early exploration, a theme that would echo through subsequent scholarship.

The excitement surrounding the map's discovery also sparked a renaissance of interest in other historical artifacts, leading to a greater appreciation for the cartographic history of the Ottoman Empire. Scholars began to re-evaluate the narratives that shaped early explorations and the geopolitical landscape of the time, urging a second look at the interconnectedness of empires and cultures that were historically compartmentalized.

Through the lens of the Piri Reis Map, modern researchers recognized the critical importance of integrating narratives that honor indigenous knowledge systems and the myriad contributions of different cultures to the development of global geography. The discovery thus transcended the mere unveiling of an object; it reignited discussions around collaboration, connection, and the democratic nature of knowledge production.

In essence, the discovery of the Piri Reis Map symbolized the unearthing of a rich tapestry woven from the threads of exploration, culture, and knowledge exchange. It challenged historians and cartographers alike to consider how they perceive the past. The map continues to serve as an invitation to explore the complexities of our shared history, urging us to grapple with our evolving understandings of geography, culture, and the inexhaustible curiosity that fuels human exploration. The moment it was discovered, it immediately became a pivotal artifact, providing insight not just into Ottoman mapping practices but also into the broader narrative of humanity's quest for understanding the world we inhabit.

4.2. Intricate Details and Annotations

The Piri Reis Map stands as a testament not only to exemplary cartography of its time but also to the intricate artistry and detailed knowledge embedded within its creation. A closer examination of its visual and textual elements reveals an artistry that blends accuracy with imagination, showcasing Piri Reis's profound understanding of geography and culture. Each line, flourish, and annotation on the map serves a dual role: it offers navigational information while also weaving a narrative of exploration.

At the core of the map's design are the meticulous depictions of coastlines, islands, and significant landmarks derived from both firsthand observations and earlier cartographic sources. While constructing his map, Piri Reis navigated the delicate balance between aesthetics and functionality, ensuring that while the map could serve as a reliable guide, it also captivated its viewers. The vibrant colors used to illustrate landforms and water bodies not only demarcate territory but also evoke a sense of wonder, drawing viewers into a world of exploration and discovery.

Annotations on the map are equally fascinating, displaying a myriad of information that showcases the cultural and historical context of the era. Piri Reis included texts that identify various geographic features, along with notes on local peoples and potential trade routes —each annotation reflecting an ethos of knowledge-sharing. This meticulous attention to detail signals his devotion to the craft of mapmaking, as he not only chronicled the landscape but also created a living document that encapsulated contemporary understandings of the world.

The map's embellishments also embrace artistic influences that echo the synthesis of cultures within the Ottoman Empire. Intricate borders and illustrations of fantastical sea creatures abound, conveying both a sense of the unknown and a commentary on the narratives of exploration that filtered through the 16th-century mindset. Such representations highlight the interplay between factual and mythical elements, which were often woven together as explorers sought to articulate their understanding of the diverse and largely uncharted regions they encountered.

As we explore the integrated visual and textual details of the Piri Reis Map, we find ourselves not simply observing a historical artifact but engaging with a rich tapestry of knowledge where science meets art. The map offers insights into the human drive for exploration, revealing a complex confluence of historical consciousness, technological advancement, and cultural exchange that characterized this pivotal moment in the history of cartography.

A careful dissection of these elements not only unveils the skill of Piri Reis as a cartographer but also reflects the broader narrative of the intersection between various civilizations as they engaged in the shared pursuit of discovery and understanding. This map serves as a magnificent window into an interconnected world, inviting contemporary viewers to reflect on the enduring legacy of exploration and cartography.

4.3. Artistic Influences

The Piri Reis Map serves as a striking intersection of artistry and science, showcasing the profound influence of various artistic traditions through its elaborate design and illustrative elements. To appreciate the depth of this cartographic achievement, it is essential to recognize the diverse artistic influences that Piri Reis incorporated into his work, reflecting the Ottoman Empire's rich cultural heritage and the broader intellectual currents of the 16th century.

The map is adorned with intricate borders and detailed illustrations that are emblematic of the artistic style of the time. These embellishments not only serve a decorative purpose but also function to convey a sense of the fantastical and the exotic. The incorporation of ornate borders, complete with floral motifs and geometric patterns characteristic of Islamic art, showcase the cultural identity of the Ottoman Empire. While Western cartography during this period often leaned towards practicality and precision, the Piri Reis Map balances functionality with aesthetic appeal, embodying the Ottoman tradition of integrating artistry into practical works.

One of the most notable artistic influences evident in the Piri Reis Map comes from the artistic traditions of Persian miniatures. The detailed representations of landscapes and cities evoke the eloquent, miniature paintings found in Persian art. These illustrations not only demonstrate Piri Reis's keen observational skills but also draw upon a rich visual vocabulary that resonates with viewers on both artistic and cultural levels. The inclusion of ships navigating the oceans and the whimsical depictions of sea creatures further enrich the map's narrative, illustrating the marriage of mythology and reality in the exploration of the unknown. Such representations evoke the sense of adventure that characterized the Age of Discovery, capturing the spirit of exploration that was alive during the early 1500s.

Additionally, the map's layout reflects the influence of Mediterranean navigational practices that would have been familiar to Piri Reis. The depiction of coastlines and maritime routes displays not just geographical accuracy but also an understanding of trade winds, currents, and regional characteristics that were critical for mariners of the era. These elements underscore an artistic sensibility that draws from both empirical observations and established conventions in navigation. The blend of scientific observation with artistic design is a hallmark of Renaissance humanism, exemplifying a shift towards an integrative approach to knowledge that encompassed both the empirical and the interpretative.

The Piri Reis Map also bears the marks of intercultural exchange characteristic of the late medieval and early modern periods. The cartographic work encompasses contributions not only from Ottoman sources but also from the rich intellectual traditions of Greece, Rome, and the Islamic Golden Age. This synthesis reflects a broader artistic and scholarly milieu where knowledge was shared among cultures, fostering a collaborative spirit that transcended geographical boundaries. By drawing from a diverse array of sources, Piri Reis crafted a map that became an emblem of cultural identity and a testament to the collaborative intellectual aspirations of various civilizations.

Furthermore, the fantastical elements depicted in the map—ranging from mythical sea monsters to elaborate renditions of animals—offer insight into how explorative narratives shaped perceptions of the world. These artistic licenses reflect the fervent imagination of explorers who ventured into the unknown, encapsulating a blend of fear, wonder, and curiosity that characterized the act of exploration. Piri Reis's integration of such elements serves to highlight the significance of storytelling in cartography, where maps were not merely functional tools but also cultural artifacts imbued with narrative significance.

In summary, the artistic influences evident in the Piri Reis Map reveal a complex interplay between artistry, culture, and science. Drawing upon the rich artistic heritage of the Ottoman Empire alongside a broader Mediterranean tradition, Piri Reis created a cartographic masterpiece that transcended conventional mapping practices of its time. The intricate designs, detailed illustrations, and incorporation of mythical elements not only provide a glimpse into the geographical knowledge of the era but also encapsulate the spirit of exploration and cultural exchange that defined the Age of Discovery. As we engage with the Piri Reis Map, we uncover layers of meaning that speak to our shared human narrative—one that continues to inspire curiosity and wonder across generations.

4.4. Comparisons with Contemporary Maps

The Piri Reis Map, created in 1513, represents a seminal moment in the history of cartography, not only for its artistic merit but also for its ambitious scope. To fully grasp its significance, it's crucial to compare and contrast it with contemporary maps produced during the same era. This examination reveals the prevailing techniques, cartographic philosophies, and geographical understanding of the time, shedding light on how the Piri Reis Map stands apart from its counterparts.

During the early 16th century, European cartography was undergoing a dramatic transformation propelled by the Age of Discovery. European explorers were charting new territories, and their experiences were reflected in maps that grew increasingly detailed and expansive. Piri Reis, as an Ottoman cartographer, positioned himself within this broader context, showcasing landmasses in a way that mirrored the artistic and scientific ambitions of European mapmakers while also being informed by the rich tradition of Islamic scholarship.

Contemporary maps from Europe, such as those produced by Gerardus Mercator and Martin Waldseemüller, utilized advancements in navigation and ship design that enabled new explorations. For instance, Mercator's famous projection, introduced later in the 16th century, focused on maintaining direction, making it ideal for navigation despite distorting the size of terrestrial areas near the poles. In contrast, the Piri Reis Map emphasizes a more artistic rendering of the world, blending accurate outline sketches of coastlines with mythological and decorative elements. This gives Piri Reis's creation a unique character that raises questions about the blending of navigational functionality and artistic expression.

One of the most striking differences can be found in the maps' treatment of South America. Contemporaneous European maps tended to focus on the Iberian conquests, emphasizing coastal features, trade routes, and imperial interests. The Piri Reis Map, however, offers a broader geographical representation that includes both well-known territories such as the Caribbean and speculative depictions of lands yet to be fully explored. Piri Reis's choice to incorporate regions inferred through second-hand accounts illustrates an audacity in cartography that was not universally adopted by his contemporaries. His map acknowledges the complexity of geographic knowledge as it stood at the time, melding the known with regions that remained ambiguous and unexplored.

Additionally, the annotations on the Piri Reis Map, which identify various peoples, locations, and possible resources, diverge from the sometimes sparse texts found on European counterparts. The Piri Reis Map seemingly invites its viewers to engage with a larger narrative; geographical knowledge is inseparable from the cultures inhabiting those lands. This contrasts with the often more utilitarian approach taken by European mapmakers, who might focus on showing land purely for navigational utility without providing the same contextual narrative.

In terms of mythical and allegorical representation, the Piri Reis Map is richly adorned with images of sea monsters and fantastical creatures, which reflect not only the cartographic norms of the period but also the meld of observable realities and the imaginative narratives that explorers often spun to convey their experiences at sea. While European maps began gravitating towards more empirical portrayals, the Piri Reis Map retains a sense of wonder and the fantastic that aligns with the storytelling tradition prevalent in Islamic art and scholarship.

Furthermore, contemporary European maps often functioned as tools of political power and colonial ambition, necessarily narrowing their focus on territories that directly pertained to imperial interests. The Piri Reis Map, with its wider portrayal of the globe, emphasizes the interconnectedness of cultures in a thriving Mediterranean world. It reflects the Ottoman Empire's own aspirations on the global stage—an ambition that included not just the acquisition of territory but an enriched understanding of the world itself.

As we draw these comparisons, we begin to recognize that the Piri Reis Map acts as both a mirror and a complement to contemporary

European cartography. It highlights a moment in history where cross-cultural exchanges were sweeping, bridging gaps between empirical data and narrative artistry, and fostering a more nuanced understanding of the globe. The Piri Reis Map's distinctive character lays bare the wonders and complexities of exploration during an era defined by curiosity and ambition, cementing its place as a landmark achievement in cartographic history. In this, it serves as a testament to not just the navigational aspirations of the Ottoman Empire but to the broader human quest for knowledge that transcends borders and cultures, linking us to the intricate tapestry of our shared past.

4.5. Mythical and Allegorical Elements

The Piri Reis Map is rich with mythical and allegorical elements that invite viewers to consider not only the geographical information it conveys but also the imaginative narratives that it reflects. Created in a time of exploration and discovery, the map captures the essence of an era fueled by human curiosity and intrigue about the world beyond familiar horizons. Within its intricate designs and annotations, contrasting the factual with the fantastical, Piri Reis juxtaposes observed realities with the colorful legends that traveled alongside explorers of the age.

One of the most prominent features of the Piri Reis Map is its incorporation of mythical sea creatures and elaborate illustrations that echo the artistic traditions of the Islamic world. These fanciful representations were not merely decorative; they served a dual purpose by reflecting the collective psyche of society and embodying the fears and wonders of the explorers who encountered uncharted waters. Stories of mermaids, sea serpents, and other fantastic beings were prevalent among seafaring cultures and were often used to explain the dangers and mysteries of the ocean, creating a tapestry of myth interwoven with the pursuit of knowledge.

For example, the depictions of strange creatures lingering in the seas surrounding known lands can be seen as a reflection of what sailors believed they might encounter on their voyages. These illustrations communicate an essential aspect of exploration during the time—

the blend of real experiences and the mythical narratives that were borne out of unexplainable phenomena encountered at sea. Such artistic licenses helped to create a narrative around the map that captivated audiences and emphasized the brave endeavors of those who ventured into the unknown.

The map also highlights an allegorical representation of the world. The inclusion of regions that were only speculated upon, such as parts of the New World alongside established territories, indicates both the vision and ambition of cartographers like Piri Reis. These uncharted lands are tinged with an element of fantasy, suggesting an artist's interpretation of what could exist, born from stories told by sailors and explorers who returned with tales of distant shores. The map's imaginative portrayals provoke a dialogue surrounding the unknown —its incitement to explore what lies beyond the familiar landscapes, which ultimately drives the spirit of discovery.

In juxtaposition to the representations of the mythical are the historical narratives reflected in the map's cultural annotations. Piri Reis integrates information from various sources, merging his own observations with historical accounts gathered from prior expeditions and indigenous peoples. The interplay of these layers of knowledge underscores the propensity to mythologize journeys undertaken by those who braved the waters. The act of map-making becomes an allegorical quest in itself, one that preserves stories through geography, maintaining the memory of both factual lands and the legends that confirmed their allure.

The mythical and allegorical aspects of the Piri Reis Map also serve as a reminder of the limitations of 16th-century knowledge. While modern audiences may perceive maps as precise representations of geography, the realities of cartography in Piri Reis's time were much less defined. Knowledge was often based on rumor and anecdote about new lands, necessitating a blend of fact and fiction. The mythical creatures depicted function as placeholders for the unexplored, symbolizing that vast human imagination still existed amidst a burgeoning desire for empirical knowledge.

Furthermore, the intriguing amalgamation seen in the Piri Reis Map delineates how cultures interacted, often merging understanding with belief systems. Such mythical narratives traveled across cultures, leading to a homogenization of ideas that shaped perceptions about the earth and its many inhabitants. In this sense, Piri Reis's map does not just serve as navigational aid; it embodies a cultural artifact, representative of the exchanges and interconnections between diverse peoples and their languages, myths, and histories.

Ultimately, the mythical and allegorical elements of the Piri Reis Map challenge the contemporary viewer to engage with cartography not just as a record of geographical data but as a narrative woven from the fabric of cultural beliefs, experiences, and aspirations. It encourages us to reflect on how the human journey towards discovery has been fueled by a tug-of-war between the known and the unknown—a timeless curiosity that continues to propel exploration, mapping, and the stories we tell about our world. Through the lens of this remarkable map, we come to understand that every line drawn and every representation made encapsulates a wider story, merging the tangible with the mythical in the exhilarating quest for understanding.

5. Mapping the Known and the Unknown

5.1. Depictions of Africa

The depiction of Africa on the Piri Reis Map is a captivating aspect that invites both scrutiny and appreciation, especially when situated within the broader context of 16th-century cartography and exploration. It represents not just a geographic rendering but also reflects the complex interactions between European perception and indigenous understanding of the continent at the time. The intricate details that Piri Reis included offer insights into the knowledge that existed about Africa during the early 1500s, while simultaneously revealing the limitations and assumptions inherent in that knowledge.

To begin with, the representation of Africa on the Piri Reis Map is distinguished by its unique configuration. The northwestern coast, characterized by places like Tunisia and the Barbary Coast, is rendered with a degree of accuracy that indicates an awareness of both trade routes and local knowledge. Piri Reis included a number of noteworthy geographic features such as the Nile River, which flows from the interior of the continent toward the Mediterranean Sea. This demonstrates an understanding of Africa's rivers as vital arteries that not only shaped its geography but served as catalysts for trade and cultural exchange—elements that were pivotal for both local peoples and European explorers seeking new connections.

The map juxtaposes these geographic realities with certain embellishments that hint at broader cultural narratives and myths surrounding Africa at the time. For instance, the midsection and southern regions of Africa retain a degree of ambiguity, with areas that are less defined and often interpolated with conjectural information. This renders those parts of the continent as somewhat mysterious, aligning with the prevailing European attitudes toward these distant lands. The uncharted territories are depicted as vague expanses, filled with the imaginative interpretations of lands as yet unexplored.

One noteworthy aspect of the Piri Reis Map is its inclusion of mythical creatures and figures that were often imputed to the African continent by earlier travelers and scholars. The creative depictions of strange beings, particularly in coastal areas, underscore the amalgamation of fact and folklore that characterized European perceptions of Africa during this era. This representation highlights how explorers and mapmakers contended with the narrative of the "Unknown," relying on imaginative narratives to fill in gaps in their knowledge about regions they had not yet physically encountered. As such, the map serves as a testimonial to the duality of knowledge—a blend of empirical experience and mythological imagination.

Moreover, the Piri Reis Map reflects the interplay between indigenous knowledge and European exploratory frameworks. Piri Reis had access to a wealth of cartographic information from various sources, including consultations with sailors, traders, and previous explorers. This synthesis of information allowed him to include African coastal regions that were known to the Ottoman Empire, highlighting active trading routes which not only facilitated commerce but also cultural exchanges across the Mediterranean and into the Atlantic corridors. The strategic importance of regions such as Egypt reinforces how intertwined the destinies of Europe, Africa, and the Middle East became during this time of expanding maritime endeavors.

However, as we examine the map's depiction of Africa, it is crucial to recognize the limitations of the knowledge upon which it was constructed. Piri Reis's map serves as both a product of its time and an artifact that embodies the questions of knowledge production. The simplification of regions into vague outlines points to a lack of detailed understanding of Africa's interior. Europeans possessed little accurate knowledge about the vastness of the continent and the myriad cultures it housed, leading to the portrayal of areas as unexplored and often exoticized.

The challenges surrounding the representation of Africa highlight significant assumptions prevalent in European cartography of the period. The narratives that emerged from this mapping endeavor reflected cultural biases, with Africa often conceptualized as a place of mystery, untamed nature, and potential danger. Such representations were shaped by an existing European worldview that placed the continent on the periphery of both curiosity and fear, resulting in maps that illustrated that ambivalence in their departures from accuracy.

In summary, the depiction of Africa on the Piri Reis Map is emblematic of the intersection between exploration, cartography, and cultural imaginings across the 16th century. It encapsulates the complex dynamics of knowledge-sharing between European and African contexts while showcasing both the strengths and weaknesses of contemporary mapping practices. As we delve into the intricate details and representations on the Piri Reis Map, we come to appreciate how cartography serves as a compelling lens through which to explore the evolving narratives surrounding Africa, knowledge production, and the enduring legacy of exploration—a confluence of realities that continues to resonate across cultures and time.

5.2. The Enigma of Antarctica

The unexplained presence of what some interpret as the icy contours of Antarctica on the Piri Reis Map poses intriguing questions regarding our understanding of historical geography and exploration. Although the southern continent was officially discovered in the early 19th century, the map generated by Piri Reis in 1513 sparked debates that challenge traditional notions of discovery and mapping practices during the Age of Exploration. By analyzing the contours, writings, and historical context of the map, scholars have proposed various theories regarding the representation of Antarctica, potentially suggesting that the map points to a far richer tapestry of knowledge than previously considered.

The depiction of what could be interpreted as Antarctica is positioned intriguingly within the context of the Piri Reis Map. The outlines of landmasses toward the southern part of the map appear to correlate with modern understandings of the continent's coastline, even though they are presented without the ice cover that obscures it today. This raises the possibility that the information available to Piri Reis and his contemporaries was derived from earlier explorations or sources that have since been lost to history. Some theorists argue that these iterations of a southern landmass could represent a remnant of ancient knowledge, potentially pointing to retellings of earlier expeditions long before the official discovery by explorers like James Cook.

Explorative narratives often intermingle real accounts with imagination and speculation, leaving a blurred line between fact and myth. Piri Reis's methodology embodied this interplay; his work synthesized knowledge from various cultures and earlier cartographic traditions, including those from Greco-Roman and Arab sources. The presence of a southern land on his map could reflect knowledge that passed through oral traditions or explorative records that were not formally documented. The notion of polar landmasses was not exclusive to the Ottomans; it echoed through classical texts and possibly even in indigenous accounts that preceded European exploration narratives.

Another compelling aspect of this enigma is the possibility of inaccurate or divergent geographical representations. The Piri Reis Map was compiled using multiple sources—some that may have relied on conjectural data. Given the mapmaker's reliance on earlier maps, which might have included speculative landmasses based on myths or limited explorations, Piri Reis's illustrations could reflect more of an aspirational landscape than a strictly accurate one. In presenting a landmass in polar regions, he may have been contributing to the cartographic tradition of representing the "unknown" rather than providing a scientific mapping of what lay beyond the known confines of the continent's coastline.

Historians and cartographers have engaged fiercely with the implications of these interpretations. Some suggest that the knowledge depicted might also be a reflection of the empire's desire to consolidate its maritime navigation and understanding of territorial expanse. Mapping the potential of a landmass like Antarctica would symbolize an inherent interest in exploring uncharted territories and expanding the Ottoman maritime horizon across both known and speculative realms.

Moreover, adventurers of the time, particularly the Ottomans, took great interest in southern voyages, including those into the Indian Ocean and surrounding regions. This growing fascination might have encouraged the consolidation of various geographical attributes from the south, uniting both observed and theorized data into the Piri Reis Map—a key document for maritime navigation and exploration, echoing imperial aspirations and curiosity about what lay beyond the horizon.

However, the notion of a pre-discovery Antarctic has not been without criticism. Skeptics argue that the irregularities in the mapping and the inconclusive nature of the interpretations are perhaps more indicative of the conjectural practices prevalent within cartography of the period. This illustrates a critical tension in understanding historical geography; as knowledge evolved, so too did the interpretations of maps, leading to debates over the validity of existential territories.

As we contemplate the enigma of Antarctica's representation on the Piri Reis Map, it becomes clear that it acts as a portal into historical expectancies, aspirations, and the complexities of cartographic prints that attempt to minimize the vastness of the world through drawings. This point of inquiry showcases how history itself is laden with layers —each revealing the curiosity, exploration, and interpretations that do not adhere to the rigid timelines of discovery often oversimplified by modern historiography.

In essence, the cartographic mystery encoded in the Piri Reis Map invites ongoing exploration and discussion. Whether the potential representation of Antarctica reflects prior knowledge, speculation, or artistic license remains a question that resonates deeply within historical studies, offering both richness and uncertainty in our understanding of exploration narratives. As we further untangle these enigmas, the pursuit continues, reflecting humanity's perpetual yearning to chart, comprehend, and make sense of the vast and often unexplained landscapes of our world.

5.3. South America's Representation

In examining the representation of South America on the Piri Reis Map, one encounters intriguing elements that speak not only to the geographical knowledge of the early 16th century but also to the broader imperial aspirations and intercultural exchanges of the time. The map, drawn by the skilled Ottoman admiral and cartographer Piri Reis, offers a snapshot of a continent at the brink of monumental changes brought about by European exploration and conquest. As we navigate through the layers of this representation, we uncover a complex interplay of exploration, cultural narratives, and the evolving perceptions of an enigmatic land that would soon become central to global history.

The Piri Reis Map characterizes South America with remarkable detail, especially in its northern and eastern regions. The map depicts the coastline of Brazil with noteworthy accuracy for the time, suggesting an engagement with contemporary Portuguese explorations. At the time of its creation in 1513, the Portuguese, under the guidance of explorers like Pedro Álvares Cabral, had recently made landfall in Brazil, and this knowledge was likely disseminated within the networks that reached Ottoman scholars. Piri Reis's representation not only showcases the geographical layout but reflects an awareness of the burgeoning colonial interests that defined European maritime ambitions in the New World.

The depiction of the Amazon River is particularly noteworthy. The river is illustrated prominently, and its extensive network of tributaries appears to be sketched with a degree of sophistication for the period. This element serves as an indication of the importance of river systems not just as geographical features, but also as vital arteries for trade and indigenous cultures that thrived along their banks. The attention given to such features signifies Piri Reis's recognition of the intricate interconnection between landforms and the societies dependent on them, showcasing a depth of understanding that transcended mere cartographic representation.

However, the map also bears the hallmarks of speculative geography. Certain areas are rendered with less clarity, particularly the southern regions, which seem to blend into ambiguity. This vagueness speaks to an inherent challenge faced by early cartographers, who navigated the tension between observed realities and the limitations of their existing knowledge. Parts of the continent are sketched in ways that suggest imagination rather than direct observation, highlighting how the unknown often prompted speculation. Piri Reis employed a combination of legends and myths, indicative of an era when geographical ignorance was prevalent, and maps often served as canvases for both fact and imaginative storytelling.

In tandem with these observations, the presence of indigenous peoples and potential resources in the annotations surrounding the South American coastline signifies the cultural narratives that shaped the European understanding of the continent. The map includes descriptions of native populations, pointing to an interest in their lifestyles and practices, as well as the potential for resource extraction. This portrayal encapsulates a moment in history where the imperial gaze began to extend deeply into the New World, searching for knowledge, conquest, and cultural exchange. Piri Reis's annotations reflect the merging of various knowledge systems—European, indigenous, and Islamic—that characterized the early 16th century, revealing a complex tapestry of intercultural interaction and imperial ambition.

The visual representation of South America on the Piri Reis Map further complicates our understanding of cultural perceptions at the time. The map's artistic elements, which elegantly intertwine geographic accuracy with mythical embellishments, convey a collective narrative about exploration during an era defined by both wonder and danger. Piri Reis utilized an imaginative flair to depict the coasts and landscapes, infusing them with life and intrigue. This approach underscores how cartography was as much about storytelling as it was about navigation—a narrative drawn from the collective experiences and encounters of explorers.

Furthermore, the map's interpretation of South America provokes reflection on the broader implications for indigenous peoples. As European powers, emboldened by recent discoveries, prepared to assert their dominance over these lands, the depictions on the Piri Reis Map symbolize the transition of South America into the crosshairs of imperial conquest. The inclusivity of local knowledge, as well as the combination of observation and speculation, illustrates a reality that would soon be overshadowed by colonization and its ensuing impacts on indigenous cultures.

In conclusion, the representation of South America in the Piri Reis Map provides a fascinating glimpse into a moment on the cusp of profound geographical and cultural transformation. The combination of accuracy and speculation, the intertwining of indigenous knowledge and European ambition, and the artistic narratives woven into its design all contribute to a rich tapestry that speaks to the complexities of exploration. Piri Reis's work, thus, stands not only as a significant cartographic achievement but as a document that encapsulates the spirit of exploration, imperial aspirations, and the intricate ways in which human understanding of the world was continually reshaped during the Age of Discovery. As we reflect on this representation, it becomes clear that the map serves as a palimpsest—layers of knowledge, culture, and ambition written across the very contours of a continent.

5.4. Imaginary Geographies

The concept of imaginary geographies plays a significant role in the understanding and interpretation of maps throughout history, particularly in the context of the Piri Reis Map. As a creation of the early 16th century, this artistry not only reflects the geographic knowledge of its time but also reveals the powerful influences of myth, speculation, and cultural narratives that shaped the explorative spirit of the era. In analyzing the Piri Reis Map, we uncover a tapestry woven with both tangible territories and fictional lands, each representing aspirations, fears, and the human desire to understand the vast and often unfathomable world beyond the horizon.

Imaginary geographies manifest in various forms, from speculative landmasses to mythical creatures, all of which not only embellish the map but invite a deeper inquiry into the beliefs and knowledge systems of the time. The Piri Reis Map itself is replete with illustrations of idealized shores and mythical beings, which conjure images of lands inhabited by unknown peoples and cultures. This blending of reality with imagination is not merely ornamental; it signifies the way in which explorers and cartographers grappled with the mysteries of uncharted territories, often relying on stories, rumors, and extrapolations based on limited understanding.

For instance, the inclusion of regions that existed only in the imagination was not uncommon in cartography of the period. Such hypothetical spaces would fill areas that were inadequately mapped or entirely uncharted, serving as placeholders for the unknown. Within the Piri Reis Map, we might encounter outlines of territories that bear resemblance to real locations but are interspersed with elements that speak to the lore and mythology that navigators carried with them. This intertwining of fact and fiction reflects an era steeped in exploration, where the act of mapping was inherently tied to the vast imagination of its creators.

The imaginary geographies found in the Piri Reis Map illuminate the dynamic interplay between cultural narratives and empirical geographic knowledge. The historical context of early 16th-century exploration is characterized by a burgeoning desire for knowledge that existed alongside significant gaps in understanding. As European powers sough New World territories, they encountered indigenous cultures and ecosystems that challenged preconceived notions. The vastness of the Americas called for imaginative mapping practices; therefore, geographic representations could not be wholly accurate, instead needing to rely on narrative embellishment to narrate tales of discovery.

Moreover, the practice of infusing maps with allegorical elements was widespread, as these additions served not only aesthetic purposes but philosophical ones as well. The powerful narratives surrounding geography are often imbued with moral and social meanings, reflecting how different cultures perceived themselves in relation to the unknown. The stories told through the Piri Reis Map, embellished with artistic representations and mythical allusions, were lenses that shaped the worldview of contemporaneous societies—a confluence of aspiration, dread, and wonder surrounding the exploration of lands beyond the known world.

Maps can also serve as a canvas for political aspirations; the physical representation of land can reflect territorial claims and national ambitions. In the case of the Piri Reis Map, the inclusion of imaginary geographies alongside accurate depictions highlights an Ottoman desire to assert its maritime dominance. By weaving together fact and myth, Piri Reis crafted a narrative that illustrated the empire's reach and intellectual prowess while simultaneously inviting contemplation about potential endeavors beyond the immediate horizons.

The exploration of imaginary geographies also invites an interrogation of historical narratives around discovery. The complexities of cultural encounters with lands filled with unknowns often favored European savants, overshadowing the rich histories of indigenous peoples whose knowledge systems and narratives were frequently marginalized in the wake of colonization. Thus, the mythical elements embedded in maps can be seen as both powerful storytelling devices and encapsulations of historical injustices.

Ultimately, the imaginary geographies represented in the Piri Reis Map are a testament to the cartographer's craft—a sophisticated blending of observation and creativity driven by humanity's enduring urge to venture forth and explore. By piecing together knowledge from diverse sources while embracing the possibility of the unknown, Piri Reis allowed for a broader comprehension of the world that transcended mere geographical representation. Each imaginative depiction invites contemporary viewers to engage thoughtfully with the past, acknowledging the complexities inherent in the processes of discovery and the mapping of human experience. Through examining these imaginary landscapes, we cultivate a deeper understanding of the intricate relationship between knowledge, exploration, and the human spirit that has defined cartography throughout the ages.

5.5. Omissions and Alterations

The Piri Reis Map serves as a remarkable artifact illustrating the intricate balance between knowledge and speculation that characterized map-making during the early 16th century. Within this context, omissions, alterations, and modifications on the map reveal critical gaps in understanding, cultural interpretations, and the aspirations of explorers during this time. By examining these elements closely, we uncover the multilayered narrative of exploration, knowledge acquisition, and the limitations faced by cartographers as they graphed uncharted territories.

Central to the discussion of omissions in the Piri Reis Map is the acknowledgment of the limitations of knowledge at the time. As Piri Reis synthesized information from multiple sources—some derived from firsthand experience and others from secondhand accounts—certain areas of the map reveal a lack of clarity or detail. This vagueness is particularly evident in the regions that lay outside the primary navigation routes—such as portions of the South American coastline and areas of the interior continent itself. The absence of thorough representations of these landscapes indicates a reliance on incomplete or speculative information, revealing a world that was much larger than the mapmaker could accurately portray.

Moreover, the map's depiction of South America and the Caribbean showcases an interesting juxtaposition between known and unknown territories. While certain areas, such as Brazil and the Gulf of Mexico, are rendered with surprising detail and accuracy given the cartographic practices of the period, other regions appear as vague outlines or are altogether omitted from the depiction. This contrast highlights how explorers often prioritized regions of immediate interest or utility—such as trade routes and vital trading ports—while less well-known areas remained ignored, reflecting the immediate geopolitical interests of the Ottoman Empire.

Additionally, the way in which the map incorporates mythical figures and imaginative elements serves to further highlight omissions in empirical knowledge. Piri Reis embellished his map with illustrations of sea monsters and fantastical landscapes, which not only told a story of exploration but filled gaps in geographical understanding with fantastical interpretations. These mythical inclusions may suggest an attempt to invoke a sense of the unknown—providing viewers with a narrative of adventure while simultaneously confronting the limitations of factual representation.

Another notable alteration within the Piri Reis Map is its projection and arrangement of landmasses, which often differ from the established geographic visualizations of the time. The method of presenting particular regions diverges from empirical cartographic standards. For instance, some territories are oriented in a manner that does not adhere to conventional north-south or east-west dimensionality. This alteration can be interpreted as a product of the constraints faced by early cartographers, who were striving to communicate a vast and complex world but often lacked access to accurate methods and consistent information that would enable a singular, standardized representation.

The Santiago Bay area, for instance, appears heavily altered, showcasing inaccuracies in the layout of the coastline that might stem from a combination of disparate sources. Such modifications bring to light the challenging nature of synthesis in cartography, reflecting how even the best-informed cartographers grappled with information discrepancies. Through alterations, Piri Reis demonstrates an effort to create a cohesive representation of the world as it was understood —however imperfectly—while also acknowledging the multitude of influences that contributed to that understanding.

Importantly, omissions on the Piri Reis Map also reflect broader cultural narratives, including the perspectives and experiences of indigenous peoples. In areas where local populations existed, there is often a lack of representation or inadequate acknowledgment of their presence. This oversight hints at the dynamics of power and imperial ambition that characterized the period, where the focus was primarily placed on land acquisition and potential resources, rather than understanding or documenting the societies that inhabited those lands.

The intricate relationship between geographic accuracy and cultural depictions within the map underscores the inherent biases that shaped its creation. While Piri Reis sought to document knowledge through navigation and cartography, the intentions behind his omissions and alterations offer deeper insight into how knowledge was constructed in the service of particular geopolitical narratives. In doing so, the Piri Reis Map serves as a reflection of its time—illustrating the spirit of exploration while exposing the limits of a nascent global understanding in the 16th century.

In summary, the omissions and alterations found within the Piri Reis Map unveil the complexities and challenges of early cartographic practices. The interplay between observed realities and imaginary constructs presents a profound opportunity to engage with the broader narratives of exploration, imperial ambition, and cultural interactions during a transformative period in history. As we navigate through these gaps in knowledge, we not only gain insight into the limitations of the map itself but also reflect upon the continuing evolution of geographic understanding and the ongoing dialogue about how humanity chooses to map its world and its experiences. Ultimately, the Piri Reis Map serves as both a document of its time and a doorway into the ongoing journey of discovery, learning, and the ever-expanding quest to understand the world around us.

6. The Cartographer's Craft: Techniques and Tools

6.1. Compass, Quadrant, and Astrolabe

The tools of the trade for 16th-century cartographers, particularly in the context of the Piri Reis Map, reflect a fascinating interplay of tradition, innovation, and the spirit of exploration that characterized the Age of Discovery. Among these instruments, the compass, quadrant, and astrolabe stand out as crucial devices that provided the navigational guidance necessary for both sea voyages and map-making. Each instrument contributed significantly to the accuracy and functionality of maps during this transformative period in history.

The compass, an invention borrowed from China, became an indispensable navigational tool for European explorers sailing into uncharted waters. This device enabled mariners to determine cardinal directions regardless of visibility, thus allowing them to maintain a consistent course even during periods of low visibility or stormy weather. For Piri Reis and his contemporaries, the compass offered a reliable sense of orientation, enhancing their confidence as they traversed vast and unknown seas. The presence of the compass in maritime traditions marked a shift in oceanic navigation, as it allowed explorers to venture farther into the horizon, paving the way for new discoveries and charting practices.

Complementing the compass was the quadrant, a device primarily used for measuring the altitude of celestial bodies above the horizon. This instrument provided vital information regarding latitude, allowing navigators to ascertain their position relative to the equator. By calculating the angle of the sun at midday or the altitude of stars at night, sailors could pinpoint their latitude with increasing accuracy, which was essential for effective navigation. Piri Reis's ability to blend empirical data with navigational instruments reflects the broader shift towards scientific observation in cartography, a hallmark of Renaissance thought.

Equally pivotal was the astrolabe, another ancient device that played a significant role in maritime navigation. Astrolabes allowed users to measure the angle of the sun and stars above the horizon, crucial for determining both latitude and time. By employing this device, navigators could perform calculations that revealed their positions on the globe. While astrolabes were more complex and required a certain level of mathematical understanding, their use among skilled navigators like Piri Reis underscored the integration of scientific inquiry into the art of cartography. The refinement of astrolabe techniques enhanced the precision of mapping efforts, allowing for more accurate representations of newly discovered territories.

Collectively, these tools—compass, quadrant, and astrolabe—not only transformed the practice of navigation but also influenced the methodologies employed by map-makers. The combination of celestial navigation and terrestrial observations led to maps that connected navigational knowledge with geographic representation, enriching the intellectual landscape of the time. Piri Reis harnessed these instruments to create his map, merging rigorous scientific observation with the imaginative art of mapping. His work exemplifies how navigational advancements prompted a renaissance in cartographic practices, facilitating the interplay between empirical knowledge and artistic representation that became pivotal in the mapping of both the known and unknown parts of the world.

Additionally, the prominent role of these tools in shaping the methods and practices of maritime exploration signified an important intellectual shift—a move from mythological understandings of geography to a more empirical, measured approach. As explorers utilized these navigational instruments to venture into unknown waters, their subsequent findings resonated through the world of cartography, enabling matters of precision and expanding human understanding of the globe.

Ultimately, the compass, quadrant, and astrolabe served as foundational instruments in the cartographic revolution of the 16th century. They enabled explorers and map-makers like Piri Reis not only to navigate with greater confidence but also to document their findings in innovative and meaningful ways. The legacy of these devices is woven into the fabric of the Piri Reis Map, underscoring the enduring spirit of exploration, scientific inquiry, and artistic ambition that characterized this transformative period in human history.

6.2. The Role of Scaling and Projections

Scaling and projections in the context of the Piri Reis Map represent a critical interplay between technical precision and artistic expression, vital for accurately rendering the complexities of three-dimensional terrains onto two-dimensional surfaces. In an era marked by burgeoning exploration and scientific inquiry, the techniques employed by cartographers like Piri Reis would evolve in response to the demands of navigation, the pursuit of accuracy, and the aesthetic considerations of map-making.

At the core of any cartographic endeavor lies the challenge of scale—the relationship between the distance on the map and the actual distance on the Earth. During the early 16th century, cartographers employed various methods to establish scale, relying on the knowledge of distances gained through navigation. One of the primary techniques involved the use of a reference grid to divide the map into manageable sections, enabling the mapping of specific regions in relation to one another. This approach allowed for the effective representation of either vast expanses or narrow coastal areas, as sailors needed to possess a clear sense of distance when traversing the waters.

Piri Reis navigated this complexity by integrating contemporary measurements of coastal outlines obtained from a variety of sources, blending these with his own observations collected during his expeditions. The scales employed on the Piri Reis Map serve as a testament not only to the quality of the navigational data available at the time but also to the adaptability of the cartographer in navigating the existing knowledge landscape. By accurately gauging distances and proportions, Piri Reis offered a map that not only catered to the navigational needs of the Ottoman Empire but also stood as a symbolic representation of the empire's ambitions.

Projections, on the other hand, introduced another layer of complexity to cartographic representation. Whereas the Earth is an imperfect sphere, cartographers have long grappled with the challenge of representing three-dimensional objects on two-dimensional planes. During Piri Reis's time, the most common approach involved using simple cylindrical projections, which could introduce distortions, especially as one moved away from the center of the projection. Elevation variations and curved coastlines became points of contention, as the act of mapping required a careful balance between artistic interpretation and the scientific endeavor for accuracy.

In the case of the Piri Reis Map, elements of projection reveal the cartographer's intent to reflect not only the actual features of the land but also the prevailing worldview and geographical understanding of the era. The southern regions displayed on the map demonstrate a simplified approach to portraying uncharted territories, often blending imagination with observed realities. This blending reflects both the limitations of knowledge regarding distant lands and the creative license exercised by Piri Reis who sought to weave together a cohesive narrative of exploration.

The advancements in cartographic techniques, such as triangulation and interpolation, were beginning to emerge during this period. However, these were not yet widely disseminated among users of maps, particularly in regions such as the Ottoman Empire. Instead, careful calculations regarding scale and allocation of space on maps depended largely on prior maps and existing navigational knowledge. Piri Reis's own practices bridged these advancements with existing methodologies, showcasing a nuanced understanding of geographical representation that wasn't solely focused on accuracy but also on usability.

As observers of the Piri Reis Map reflect on these scaling and projection techniques, it becomes evident that they served not solely as mechanical tools for navigation but also as a lens through which understanding geography and human ambition could be interpreted. The map's intricate drawings, placed in relation to its scale, conjured visions of exploration, cultural exchange, and imperial aspirations. Piri Reis's deft handling of these techniques was an early indication of the merging of art and science in cartography—a phenomenon that not only defined the practices of the time but has echoed through subsequent generations of map-making.

In conclusion, the techniques of scaling and projections in the Piri Reis Map highlight a pivotal moment in the evolution of cartography. The balance between empirical observations and artistic representations reveals Piri Reis's mastery of geographical rendering while capturing the intricacies of the observable world and the mysteries it still held. As cartographers seek to navigate the realms of the known and unknown, the legacy of such techniques, as embodied in the Piri Reis Map, continues to inspire a deeper quest for understanding geography and humanity's unending curiosity to explore and document the vast spaces we inhabit.

6.3. Materials: From Parchment to Ink

The process of creating maps in the early 16th century was as much an art form as a technical endeavor, with an array of materials playing a pivotal role in the craftsmanship that produced such intricate and informative works like the Piri Reis Map. This examination of materials takes us on a journey from the parchment used as a canvas to the inks that provided vibrant colors, each element reflecting the standards of the time and the skilled hands of the cartographer who wielded them.

At the core of the map-making process was parchment, a material derived mainly from animal hides, particularly sheepskin, goatskin, or calfskin. The choice of parchment was critical, as it needed to be durable and capable of withstanding the test of time. The preparation of parchment involved a meticulous process of cleaning, soaking, and stretching the hides to create a smooth surface. This procedure required a deft touch, ensuring the final product was uniformly thin, allowing for clear writing and detailing of cartographic features.

Parchment had advantages over paper, particularly in terms of durability and resistance to wear. In a time when navigation and exploration were fraught with peril, maps needed to endure the elements, the creaks of ship decks, and the hands of navigators poring over their details. The use of high-quality parchment in the Piri Reis Map exemplifies the level of care and intent in its creation, reflecting the significance of the artifact as a navigational tool and as a piece of artistic expression.

In addition to parchment, the inks and pigments employed in the map's creation played a crucial role in the visual impact of the cartographic work. During the early 1500s, ink production was both an artisanal craft and a science. The inks used in cartography were typically carbon-based for black inks, made from soot combined with water and a binding agent such as gum arabic. This combination produced a rich black ink that could withstand the test of time.

Colored inks were derived from various natural sources. Radix rubia (madder root) and several forms of ochre provided vibrant reds and yellows, while blues often came from lapis lazuli or indigo. The careful selection of these pigments not only served aesthetic purposes, such as delineating geographic boundaries, rendering coastlines, and providing visual motifs, but it also conveyed cultural significance. The colors became symbolic, adding layers of interpretation to the mapping of territories and denoting cultural identities present within the landscape.

The application of inks too was an art in itself, completed with the use of carefully crafted brushes made from various fibers or hair, meticulously shaped for detail and precision. Piri Reis's skills extended to the brush strokes that brought life to his map, allowing for embellishments and illustrations that interwove mythical elements alongside navigational data. The aesthetic qualities of ink usage could dramatically enhance the map's overall readability, with color coordinating elements that highlighted key features such as trade routes, coastal areas, and territories marked for exploration.

Moreover, the tools of the cartographer went beyond simple brushes and inks. The use of compasses for drawing precise circles and the stylus for incising details into the parchment highlighted a meticulous approach to creating maps. Piri Reis, as a skilled navigator and cartographer, would have been intimately familiar with these tools and their application, integrating them into his workflow to ensure accuracy in mapping the intricate contours of coastlines and other significant features.

The combination of materials utilized in the production of the Piri Reis Map—high-quality parchment, vibrant inks, and precision tools—culminated in a work that embodied both form and function. Such materials not only rendered the map a reliable navigational aid for the Ottoman Navy but also transformed it into a piece of artistic craftsmanship that captured the spirit of the Age of Exploration. The map stands as a testament to the synthesis of artistic endeavor and scientific inquiry, bridging the gap between the practical needs of navigation and the aesthetics of geographical representation.

In examining materials from parchment to ink through the lens of the Piri Reis Map, we unearth not just the technical aspects of cartography—it is a recognition of the dedication to knowledge, beauty, and human ambition that strove to chart the world's mysteries and complexities. The story of these materials reflects a rich tapestry of history, artistry, and exploration that echoes throughout the timeless quest to understand and navigate our world.

6.4. Navigational Observations

Navigational observations form a crucial aspect of understanding the Piri Reis Map's construction and its significance in the context of early 16th-century exploration. The emphasis on accurate celestial and coastal observations in the creation of maps like that of Piri Reis not only highlights the craft of cartography but also reflects the broader intellectual currents of the Age of Discovery, where exploration was fueled by a desire to navigate the vast unknowns of the world.

As a navigator and cartographer, Piri Reis was deeply aware of the importance of celestial navigation. This method, which involves using celestial bodies such as stars, the sun, and the moon to ascertain one's position at sea, was foundational for mariners of the time. The astrolabe and quadrant—both advanced navigational instruments—were essential tools for measuring the angle of celestial bodies above the horizon. With these instruments, navigators could determine their latitude, which was critical for plotting courses across the oceans.

Piri Reis, utilizing these navigational techniques, created a map that integrated not just geographical information but also astronomical calculations. His reliance on the positions of the stars and the sun allowed him to document sailing routes with remarkable accuracy for his time. During voyages, sailors would observe the position of the North Star at night or the zenith of the sun at noon to establish their latitudinal position. Such observations were meticulously recorded and noted on navigational charts, serving as guides for future journeys. By embedding such navigational observations within the Piri Reis Map, Piri Reis facilitated the practical utility of his work, enabling mariners to traverse uncharted waters confidently.

Coupled with celestial observations were the critical coastal observations that further contributed to the map's accuracy. Coastal navigation relied heavily on the characteristics of shorelines, tidal patterns, and local landmarks. Piri Reis amassed a wealth of knowledge gained from his own maritime experiences and incorporated information gathered from earlier navigators, both Ottoman and European. As he sailed along coastlines, he would meticulously document the contours of land, noting significant features such as capes, bays, and river estuaries, all of which served as visual references that guided ships as they approached land.

The representation of South America on the Piri Reis Map exemplifies how coastal observations interplayed with navigational practice.

The map reveals detailed outlines of the Brazilian coastline, mapping notable rivers like the Amazon with impressive accuracy, indicative of firsthand observations augmented by accounts from earlier explorers. Such precise delineation of coastlines was essential, as mariners relied on these visual cues to prevent shipwrecks and navigate treacherous waters.

Moreover, the incorporation of indigenous knowledge from encounters with local populations contributed to enriching Piri Reis's understanding of coastal features and navigational hazards, providing a more comprehensive picture of the territories he mapped. These interactions reflected not only a synthesis of various knowledge systems but also an acknowledgment of the diversity that existed in the regions being charted.

The significance of navigational observations lies not only in their immediate utility but also in their broader implications for the geopolitics of the time. As European powers sought to chart new territories and claim dominion over the New World, maps became instruments of both exploration and conquest. Piri Reis's mapping efforts, driven by both empirical observations and cultural exchanges, enabled the Ottoman Empire to assert its presence in global sea routes and affirm its intellectual authority.

While the Piri Reis Map encapsulates the navigational techniques of the early 16th century, it also serves as a narrative artifact, echoing the ceaseless curiosity and ambition of humanity to explore the unknown. The blend of celestial and coastal observations integrates scientific accuracy with artistic expression, demonstrating that maps were more than mere navigational tools; they represented complex interrelations between observation, culture, and geopolitical aspirations.

Through the lens of navigational observations, the Piri Reis Map stands as a testament to the craft of its creator and the broader context of exploration during this transformative age. As we continue to investigate navigation's central role in early cartography, we unravel not only the technical mastery of map-making but also the enduring legacy of human inquiry that continues to propel exploration and knowledge. The intrinsic relationship between observation and representation encapsulated in the Piri Reis Map solidifies its standing as a landmark achievement, one that nourishes our understanding of the world and the sophisticated practices of those who sought to chart it.

6.5. Evolution of Geographical Thought

The evolution of geographical thought from antiquity to the early modern period is a profound journey reflecting humanity's efforts to understand and describe the world. This evolution has been significantly influenced by cultural exchanges, navigational advancements, and philosophical inquiries that culminated in the making of maps, such as the Piri Reis Map. The history of cartography can be characterized by the interplay between empirical observations and the imaginative interpretations of the unknown, leading to remarkable transformations in how societies engaged with geography.

In the ancient world, geographical thought was heavily rooted in mythology and cosmology. Early maps, like those created by the Babylonians and Greeks, intertwined geographic knowledge with cultural beliefs and narratives. The ancient Greeks, particularly Ptolemy, revolutionized cartography by introducing a more systematic approach, characterized by latitudinal and longitudinal coordinates. Ptolemy's compilations represented a shift towards a more empirical understanding of geography, setting the groundwork for subsequent map-making traditions.

However, the medieval period saw a decline in this empirical approach, often leading to maps that prioritized allegorical representations over geographical accuracy. The mappa mundi of the medieval era, for instance, centered on religious beliefs, depicting the world in a way that reflected the theological and cosmological understanding of the time rather than realistic geography. This blend of geography with cultural and religious narratives illustrates how mapping served not only as a navigational tool but also as a means of understanding one's place in the universe.

The Age of Discovery marked a pivotal change in geographical thought, initiating a period dominated by exploration and the mapping of uncharted territories. European powers, especially Spain and Portugal, propelled the quest for knowledge about the New World, driven by not only economic ambitions but also a growing curiosity about distant lands and peoples. The significance of empirical observations surged as explorers returned with detailed accounts of newly discovered territories, prompting mapmakers to integrate these findings with existing knowledge.

Piri Reis, operating within this evolving framework, synthesized a wealth of navigational information from diverse sources. His map, created in 1513, serves as a testament to this transition. It exemplifies a progressive fusion of empirical observation and speculative geography, showcasing both confidence in navigational techniques and an acknowledgment of the unknown. Piri Reis's meticulous depictions reflect a sophisticated understanding of continental configurations, shape, and coastal features gained through firsthand experiences and accumulated information.

This period also witnessed a reinvention of the worldviews shaped by early maps. The mere act of mapping became a powerful tool in asserting knowledge, authority, and cultural identity. The Piri Reis Map, with its intricate details and annotations, illustrates how geography was not just a tool for navigation but also a means of legitimizing claims to new territories—a sacred right of the empire to stake its dominance on the global stage.

As cartography evolved, so did the relationship between knowledge and power. The maps created during this time were imbued with imperial motives, wherein the representation of land extended beyond mere observation into realms of political and cultural assertion. The Piri Reis Map emerges from this intersection, revealing not only geographical knowledge but also the aspirations of the Ottoman Empire laid atop the newly charted landscapes of exploring the New World.

The transition from mythological and cosmological interpretations of the world to an empirical approach in map-making reflects a broader transformation in geographical thought. The integration of scientific observation alongside artistic expression, as demonstrated in the Piri Reis Map, encapsulates the complexities and aspirations of humanity's quest to describe an ever-expanding world. As exploration continued to push the boundaries of knowledge, the maps themselves began to encapsulate not solely territories but also the rich tapestry of human experience, connection, and discovery.

Ultimately, the evolution of geographical thought, as embodied in the Piri Reis Map, invites us to appreciate the intertwining narratives of culture, exploration, and human ambition. The endeavor to render the world comprehensible and navigable—through maps—remains a testament to our insatiable curiosity and our desire to document the infinite complexities of our shared existence on this planet. The legacy of this evolution paves the way for ongoing inquiries into human understanding and the nature of knowledge, prompting us to continuously redefine our mappings of both the world and ourselves.

7. Perspectives on the New World

7.1. The Old World's Knowledge

Nestled in the rich tapestry of history, the Piri Reis Map not only serves as a navigational tool from the early 16th century but represents a vibrant confluence of knowledge from diverse cultures. When we delve into the concept of "The Old World's Knowledge," we engage with an era prior to Columbus's voyages, a time when cartographic practices were steeped in historical legacy and tradition.

Prior to the grand navigational endeavors of the late 15th century, the Old World possessed a compendium of geographical understanding derived from millennia of exploration, observation, and intellectual inquiry. This legacy was firmly grounded in the works of ancient civilizations, where the interplay of cultural beliefs and empirical observations laid the foundation for cartographic expressions.

The classical knowledge of geography began with the Babylonians, who crafted early maps such as the Imago Mundi, delineating not only geographical landmarks but intertwining mythological narratives that shaped their worldviews. Such maps were more than mere representations; they were artifacts of cultural identity, merging the known with the unknown, echoing a deep human urge to make sense of one's environment. The Greeks later advanced this knowledge with rigorous frameworks, such as the writings of figures like Anaximander and Ptolemy, whose systematic methodologies transformed how geographic information was recorded and interpreted. Their contributions, particularly Ptolemy's "Geographia," introduced the concepts of latitude and longitude that would become cornerstones of later cartography.

Even as the medieval period descended upon Europe and led to a stagnation in cartographic innovation, Islamic scholars preserved and expanded upon classical geographical knowledge. Figures like Al-Idrisi and Al-Masudi synthesized prior traditions while pioneering new explorations across Africa and Asia. Their works became critical references for both navigators and scholars, enriching the understanding of vast territories that had previously remained enigmatic to Europeans.

The Old World's knowledge culminated in a vibrant intellectual environment by the time the Age of Discovery commenced. As the Iberian kingdoms sought new trade routes and territories, the pre-existing knowledge interacted with newfound maritime discoveries, birthing a renewed zeal for accurate mapping. The voyages undertaken by explorers such as Christopher Columbus and Vasco da Gama reshaped perceptions of geography, propelling European interest in the riches of Asia and the New World.

Against this backdrop, the Piri Reis Map emerges not just as an artifact of its time but as a synthesis of centuries of accumulated knowledge. Compiled in 1513, this map encapsulated both the wisdom of ancient sources and the recent experiences of explorers navigating the newly encountered lands. Through his work, Piri Reis drew upon European, Arabic, and indigenous knowledge, reflecting a collaborative spirit that sought to piece together a world expanding beyond the confines of familiar shores.

In the Old World's knowledge lies a rich interweaving of mythology, empiricism, and cultural narratives. The visual interpretations provided by early cartographers instigated dialogues about the nature of exploration, cultural identity, and political ambitions. As we reflect on the knowledge that shaped cartography before the transatlantic voyages, we acknowledge the depth and complexity of human inquiry; the Piri Reis Map stands as a testament to this intricate legacy, where exploration transcended geographical boundaries to illuminate the shared human experience spanning different cultures and epochs.

Understanding the Old World's diverse cartographic practices enhances our recognition of the challenges faced by early explorers and the richness of their narratives. Each map was a portrait not just of lands charted, but of the intellectual and cultural ambition that propelled the exploration of the known and the unknown, creating pathways for future discoveries and understanding of our world. In this way, the origins of the Piri Reis Map resonate with the foundational knowledge that predates it, serving as a bridge that connected ancient wisdom with the burgeoning spirit of exploration that dominated the early modern era.

7.2. The Iberian Influence

The Iberian Peninsula, comprising modern-day Spain and Portugal, played a pivotal role in the Age of Exploration, which redefined geographical knowledge and drastically shaped global interactions during the 15th and early 16th centuries. The impact of Iberian exploration on cartography is especially evident in artifacts like the Piri Reis Map, which synthesized the rich tapestry of navigational practices and cultural exchanges that characterized this dynamic era. As Spain and Portugal emerged as maritime powers, their ventures into newly encountered territories brought about a significant shift in how the world was mapped and understood.

The phase of exploration initiated by Iberian powers was primarily motivated by the quest for new trade routes to Asia, driven by a desire for spices, silks, and wealth. Early expeditions, like those led by Christopher Columbus under the Spanish crown and Vasco da Gama for Portugal, served not only as ambitious undertakings of discovery but also as catalysts for advancing cartographic knowledge. These explorers encountered lands unknown to Europe and returned with accounts of their findings, significantly contributing to what would become an expansive body of geographical knowledge.

The Piri Reis Map reflects this intricate tapestry of exploration, showcasing early representations of the Americas alongside the rich navigational heritage of the Old World. Piri Reis, as an Ottoman cartographer, synthesized information from various sources, including earlier Iberian maps and charts stemming from these expeditions. The map illustrates the contours of South America and the Caribbean, highlighting the infusion of knowledge and cartographic innovations brought back by Portuguese and Spanish navigators.

The Iberian influence extended beyond mere territorial representation; it also fostered the exchange of ideas and methodologies in the craft of navigation. The navigational techniques developed by Iberian explorers—encompassing the use of astrolabes, compasses, and newly refined ship designs—had significant implications for cartography. These advancements allowed for more accurate depictions of coastlines and facilitated the integration of distant lands into existing maps. Their maritime successes served to inspire other nations and fostered an environment in which the art and science of mapping flourished.

More profoundly, the impact of the Iberian ventures was not limited to the technical aspects of mapping but also encompassed philosophical shifts regarding the nature of the world. The encounters with indigenous populations and the vast landscapes of the New World prompted cartographers to reconsider their established worldviews. The Piri Reis Map, with its blend of observed and speculative representations of the Americas, encapsulates this collision of old and new geographies, illustrating how exploration upended traditional notions of space and belonging.

The Iberian influence permeated through various layers of geographical thought, and its resonance can be observed in the artistic embellishments found on the Piri Reis Map. The cartographic practices of the period often combined visual artistry with practical utility—a trend established by Iberian powers intent on making their explorations both functional and engaging. The map's vibrant illustrations of flora, fauna, and mythical creatures evoke the sense of adventure that defined the Age of Discovery, reflecting how the awe of the unknown thrived alongside the rigor of navigational precision.

Moreover, the Iberian Age of Exploration served as both a model and a cautionary tale regarding the consequences of contact between cultures. As the explorers interacted with indigenous populations, their encounters varied from trade and alliances to violent conquests and exploitation, leading to dramatic shifts in local societies. These realities added layers of complexity to the narratives inscribed on maps, pushing future cartographers, including Piri Reis, to grapple with the ethical dimensions of representation.

In conclusion, the Iberian influence in the realm of exploration and cartography has left an indelible mark on the historical landscape of our understanding of the world. The synthesis of Iberian navigational knowledge, artistic expressions, and broader cultural exchanges resonate within the Piri Reis Map, exemplifying a moment of transformative change in global geography. As we engage with the historical layers woven into this artifact, we recognize how the ambitions of Iberian explorers not only reshaped maps but also redefined human connections across the continents, setting the stage for ongoing inquiries into the complexities of exploration, colonization, and cultural exchange that continue to thrive in our understandings of geography today.

7.3. The Clash of Old and New Geographies

The early 16th century was a transformative period in the creation and understanding of maps, particularly as explorers pushed the boundaries of the known world. In this evolving landscape of knowledge, the Piri Reis Map emerged as a remarkable example of the synthesis between long-held geographical traditions and fresh discoveries brought back by ambitious maritime expeditions. As Europe witnessed the Age of Discovery, characterized by a relentless drive for expansion and a thirst for knowledge, the clash between old understandings and new revelations became increasingly pronounced.

At the heart of this clash lay a dramatic rethinking of established worldviews. Centuries of acquired knowledge were upended as explorers like Columbus and Vasco da Gama ventured into uncharted territories, revealing lands that had remained mere speculations in the minds of scholars and the dreams of cartographers. The Piri Reis Map, with its intricate depictions of new coastlines and its reflections of indigenous territories, encapsulated this seismic shift. It illustrated the Portuguese and Spanish claims in the Americas while simultaneously intertwining them with the Ottoman Empire's aspirations of maritime supremacy—a visual narrative of competing interests and the evolving nature of geographic knowledge.

The integration of previously held beliefs about geography with emerging realities showcased the complexities and uncertainties inherent in cartographic practices of the time. Traditional maps often glimmered with mystique, possessing an array of mythological elements drawn from ancient cosmic interpretations. These maps tended to emphasize religious and cultural narratives over empirical data. In contrast, the voyage of European explorers prompted a burgeoning need for accuracy, leading to maps that not only highlighted newly charted regions but also grappled with the tension between the mythical image of the world and the tangible experience of navigation.

In approaching the Piri Reis Map, one cannot overlook its role in bridging the old and the new. While it retained elements reflective of earlier cartographic traditions, such as artistic embellishments and imaginative interpretations of the unknown, it also leveraged firsthand observations and navigational data that emerged from recent explorations. This intersection of history and the unfolding of new geographic realities visualized a world in flux, as various empires sought to chart and claim spaces that had only just begun to be comprehended.

Moreover, the Piri Reis Map serves as an illustration of a broader intellectual context in which knowledge systems were increasingly entwined. As explorers returned to Europe with discoveries, the old geographic paradigms began to confront new observations, leading to debates about the accuracy of established knowledge and the role of diverse cultural understandings in shaping worldviews. The effort to reconcile these differing perspectives highlighted the dynamic nature of cartography, as maps transformed from static representations influenced predominantly by classical texts into fluid documents embodying the spirit of exploration and cultural exchange.

In essence, the clash of old and new geographies as expressed in the Piri Reis Map encapsulates a pivotal turning point in the annals of mapping tradition. Through its intricate artistry and layered insights, it captures the essence of a world grappling with change—one where ancient wisdom and emerging empirical observations coalesce to create a more nuanced understanding of the globe. As we explore the significance of the Piri Reis Map within this context, we grapple not just with geometric precision but also with the cultural narratives and human aspirations that continue to resonate throughout the history of exploration and map-making, forever altering our perception of what maps mean to us as tools of navigation and vessels of knowledge.

7.4. Cultural Exchange and Expansionism

Cultural exchange and expansionism during the Age of Exploration played a pivotal role in shaping the dynamics of global interactions, profoundly impacting societies across continents. The Piri Reis Map, created in 1513, serves as a compelling lens through which we can examine these themes. Cartography during this era was not merely a technical endeavor but a reflection of imperial aspirations, artistic expression, and the synthesis of knowledge from diverse cultures. The intersection of exploration, cultural exchange, and the ambition of expansionism is vividly illustrated by Piri Reis's work, encapsulating the complexities of human experience during a time of remarkable transformation.

The maritime strategies of the Ottoman Empire positioned it at the crossroads of numerous cultures, allowing for an unparalleled flow of knowledge, goods, and ideas. The Piri Reis Map is emblematic of this cultural confluence, representing a synthesis of information gathered from European navigational charts, Arabic geographical texts, and indigenous accounts. The very act of map-making during this period became an exercise in cultural diplomacy, where cartographers like Piri Reis engaged with a wealth of information from different societies, fostering an environment conducive to the exchange of ideas and practices.

As explores navigated beyond the familiar shores of their territories, the lure of expansionism drove them to encounter new lands and peoples. This expansion was motivated not just by raw ambition but was deeply intertwined with the desire to collect knowledge about those regions. The Piri Reis Map illustrates the areas explored by these adventurers, mapping previously unknown territories while incorporating the cultural narratives and realities of the native societies encountered. The integration of indigenous knowledge within the map serves as a testament to the exchanges that occurred during these encounters, highlighting how cultural perspectives shaped the understanding of new spaces.

However, the impact of such cultural exchanges during the Age of Exploration was far from unidimensional. The arrival of foreign powers prompted profound changes in the societies they encountered. The introduction of new goods, technologies, and ideas often disrupted established ways of life, giving rise to periods of both cooperation and conflict. The Piri Reis Map captures this tension, reflecting the duality of cultural exchange; for example, while it showcases the artistic and scientific achievements of the time, it also symbolizes the imperialistic ambitions that drove the exploration of new lands.

The expansionist narratives that accompanied exploration often led to the imposition of foreign authority over indigenous populations. The consequences of these encounters were far-reaching, as European colonization frequently resulted in the displacement and marginalization of local cultures. The Piri Reis Map, while an artifact of cartographic achievement, also echoes the challenges faced by native societies as their lands were drawn into a global framework defined by empire-building and economic exploitation. The narratives preserved within the map stand as reminders of the complexities surrounding these historical interactions, prompting contemporary audiences to reflect upon the impacts of colonization and cultural exchange on indigenous peoples.

Yet, cultural exchange was not solely a one-way process. The interactions between explorers and native populations generated a rich exchange of knowledge, which sometimes led to hybrid cultures evolving in response to these encounters. The Piri Reis Map reflects this synthesis, as it not only documents new territories but also celebrates the blending of diverse influences—from the rich pictorial traditions of the Ottomans to the indigenous narratives that inform the mapping of these lands.

Furthermore, the Piri Reis Map highlights the significance of cultural exchange in the evolution of navigational practices. The Ottomans, adept at leveraging information from past civilizations, engaged with the maritime techniques of seafaring peoples, enhancing their own navigational capabilities. The map thus serves as a historical record of the growing interconnectedness of societies, revealing how the accumulation of knowledge benefited diverse cultures and facilitated greater understanding of the world.

In conclusion, the themes of cultural exchange and expansionism are intricately woven into the fabric of the Piri Reis Map, illustrating the dynamic interactions that characterized the Age of Exploration. As a product of its era, the map captures not only the ambition of explorers but also the complexities and consequences of their encounters with diverse cultures. Through examining Piri Reis's work, we gain valuable insight into the multifaceted nature of exploration and the profound impacts of cultural exchanges on societies worldwide. As we analyze historical maps such as the Piri Reis Map, we are reminded that understanding our past requires acknowledging both the triumphs of discovery and the legacies of disruption that accompanied expansionist pursuits—a narrative that continues to resonate in our ongoing dialogues about culture, history, and identity.

7.5. Legacy of Transformation

In the rich narrative of exploration and cartography, the Piri Reis Map emerges not merely as a remarkable cartographic achievement but as a potent symbol of transformation that bridges centuries of knowledge, technology, and cultural interchange. The map captures the essence of the early 16th century, a pivotal moment when humanity's understanding of the world was dramatically evolving. Its legacy of transformation delves deeply into the dialogue surrounding old geographies and new revelations, reflecting how maps serve as both mirrors of their time and catalysts for further understanding.

Piri Reis, an Ottoman admiral and cartographer, synthesized a wealth of geographical knowledge, incorporating observations garnered from various cultures and contemporary explorations. His map, completed in 1513, encapsulates not only the advancements in navigation and cartography of the time but also the burgeoning spirit of inquiry that characterized the Age of Discovery. In the context of an expanding world, the Piri Reis Map represented a geographic and intellectual leap, merging diverse streams of knowledge from European, Arab, and indigenous cultures. This synthesis marked a departure from an era dominated by mythological interpretations of the world, transitioning toward a more empirical understanding grounded in observation and exploration.

The legacy of transformation depicted in the Piri Reis Map reverberates through subsequent generations, influencing how maps were created, interpreted, and utilized in both navigational and cultural contexts. As seafaring expanded across the globe, the map served as a reference point for future explorations, illustrating the interconnectedness of different territories and peoples. The meticulous detail with which Piri Reis charted coastlines, rivers, and territorial features would inform subsequent mapmakers, encouraging them to engage in a similar synthesis of knowledge while fostering a competitive spirit among nations vying for discovery.

This legacy of transformation extends beyond mere cartographic accuracy. It fosters a narrative that underscores the fluidity of knowledge within a rapidly changing world. The Piri Reis Map illustrates how early cartography was founded on collaborative efforts and cultural exchanges, where the contributions of various civilizations converged to construct a more rounded understanding of geography. In this light, the map embodies the notion that exploration is inherently intercultural—a testament to the shared human experience of seeking out the unknown.

As the Piri Reis Map transcended its immediate purpose as a navigational tool, it has permeated the realms of history, art, and identity. The map invites ongoing discussions about representation and power dynamics, urging contemporary viewers to consider the significance of who has the authority to map the world and the implications of such practices. The dialogues initiated by analyses of the Piri Reis Map resonate today, as they highlight the importance of diversity in geographic knowledge and the need for mutual recognition of cultural contributions to the collective understanding of the world.

In stirring these discussions, the legacies of maps like that of Piri Reis challenge historical narratives and serve as tools for critical reflection. They offer insight into how humanity negotiates and reshapes its identity through geography, bringing into focus both the triumphs of discovery and the complexities of cultural encounters. The Piri Reis Map remains a powerful artifact that stimulates curiosity, horizon-broadening, and the continual unfolding of transformative stories shaped by exploration and connection.

In sum, the legacy of transformation associated with the Piri Reis Map stands as a celebration of the enduring human spirit of inquiry—an exploration that continues to inspire future generations to forge new paths in understanding the world around them. As the map expands our knowledge of the past, it invites us to engage actively with the ongoing processes of discovery, encouraging an appreciation for the intricate weaving of narratives that define our shared humanity.

8. The Art and Science of Cartography

8.1. Blending Art with Science

Blending art with science in the realm of cartography is a fascinating exploration of how human creativity converges with empirical knowledge to produce representations of our world that are both functional and aesthetically captivating. The Piri Reis Map, a landmark artifact of early 16th-century cartography, exemplifies this intricate interplay, illustrating how artistry enriches the scientific endeavor of mapping while adhering to the technical demands that navigational accuracy entails.

At its core, the creation of maps has always involved a synthesis of scientific principles and artistic vision. The former relies on a precise understanding of geography, math, and navigational techniques, while the latter draws upon visual aesthetics, cultural narratives, and the ability to evoke emotion through representation. In the case of the Piri Reis Map, the cartographer not only sought to record geographical features but also aspired to communicate the spirit of exploration that was a hallmark of his era. This duality is seen in the comprehensive representation of coastlines, rivers, and landmarks, executed with an artistic flair that gives the map a vibrancy and life that transcend mere function.

The scientific aspect of cartography in the context of the Piri Reis Map is rooted in the meticulous methods employed by navigators and map-makers of the time. Piri Reis utilized various navigational instruments—such as compasses, astrolabes, and quadrants—to gather empirical data about the world around him. The integration of these tools into the mapping process was essential for accurately determining latitudes and longitudes, as well as for plotting courses across the oceans. This precision guaranteed that, while the Piri Reis Map serves artistic purposes, it also functions as an essential navigational aid, crucial for Ottoman sailors venturing into unknown waters.

In crafting his map, Piri Reis drew not only from direct observation but also from a repository of knowledge derived from earlier maps, texts, and explorers' accounts. He blended this information into a cohesive representation, reflecting the convergence of different cartographic traditions—from European nautical charts to Arabic geographical insights. This synthesis exemplifies the scientific practice of building upon existing knowledge while expanding the horizons of understanding; yet, it is in the rendering of this information that the artistry emerges. Piri Reis infused his map with vibrant colors, intricate illustrations of natural elements, and elaborate borders, elevating it beyond a straightforward navigational tool into a work of art that captures the imaginations of its viewers.

The aesthetic appeal of the Piri Reis Map is further amplified by the inclusion of mythical creatures and allegorical motifs, weaving narratives that speak to the fears, hopes, and cultural identities of the time. This ability to transcend practical cartography and tap into the collective psyche of his contemporaries demonstrates the power of artistry in mapping. The incorporation of legends and symbols not only served decorative functions but also invited viewers to engage with the map on a deeper level, fostering dialogue about exploration and discovery.

As we reflect on the blending of art and science in the Piri Reis Map, we gain insight into broader philosophical questions about the nature of knowledge representation. Maps have long served as powerful tools for visualizing worlds, shaping perceptions, and asserting claims over territories. The artistic qualities of Piri Reis's work illuminate the fact that maps must not simply function as navigational aids; they must also bear witness to the values, ambitions, and curiosity of the societies that create them. This dual role amplifies the importance of understanding both the scientific rigor behind cartography and the cultural contexts that formed the tapestry of human exploration.

In essence, the Piri Reis Map embodies the seamless merging of artistic expression and scientific inquiry, ultimately reinforcing the idea that cartography is a multifaceted discipline. It challenges us to appreciate maps not merely as geographical representations but as cultural artifacts imbuing humanity's shared quest for knowledge. As researchers and explorers continue to study the intricate features of the Piri Reis Map, they unravel new layers of meaning that honor the spirit of discovery and creativity that persists in the ever-evolving practice of cartography today. Through this lens, we recognize the enduring significance of blending art with science—a testament to the rich tapestry that defines both mapping and the greater pursuit of understanding our world.

8.2. Symbols, Legends, and Scales

The Piri Reis Map is a compelling testament to the intricate relationship between symbols, legends, and scales that define the art of cartography. Its creation in the early 16th century bore the hallmarks of a transformative period in navigation and exploration, reflecting the convergence of artistic vision and scientific rigor. Within the map's carefully planned layout, Piri Reis employed symbols and legends that acted as navigational aids, while also imbuing the work with cultural narratives that represented the knowledge and beliefs of his time.

At the heart of the Piri Reis Map is the use of symbols, meticulously crafted to convey geographical features and navigational information. The choice and arrangement of symbols hold great significance; they create a visual language that communicates the relative importance of various elements. For instance, the use of different colors and shapes to represent land, water, and coastlines facilitates immediate recognition for those navigating through unfamiliar waters. The depiction of major rivers and harbors through distinct symbols emphasizes their importance in maritime navigation, while the addition of maritime features like current patterns and wind directions demonstrates Piri Reis's keen understanding of navigational challenges.

Moreover, the legends accompanying these symbols serve as explanatory guides for the viewer, clarifying the meanings attributed to the various icons present on the map. The careful integration of legends, drawn in elaborate scripts that adorn the borders of the Piri Reis Map, showcases a blend of artistic design and practical application. These annotations not only provide essential contextual information but also enrich the narrative of exploration, as they often include descriptions of regions, cultural references, and indigenous encounters. Through the synergy of symbols and legends, Piri Reis crafted a map that transcended its cartographic function—you find a document that narrates stories of voyages, aspirations, and realities of cultural exchange.

The scale used in the Piri Reis Map further articulates the complex relationship between distance and representation. While modern maps adhere to established principles of measurement, the cartographic scales of the 16th century were somewhat fluid, often influenced by the subjective experiences of navigators. In the Piri Reis Map, the scale is evident through a careful arrangement of ratios that communicate distances between locations, guiding sailors on their journeys. The variability in scale reflects the measurement practices of the time, highlighting the interdependence of empirical observations and individual experiences. This flexibility allowed for a sense of adaptability in navigating unknown waters, illuminating Piri Reis's dual role as both a scientist and an artist striving to translate his explorative ambitions into a tangible form.

The artistic embellishments that accompany geographic knowledge in the Piri Reis Map further underscore the power of symbols and legends in engaging viewers. The inclusion of mythological figures and intricate designs transforms the map from a mere navigational tool into a vibrant work of art that evokes feelings of wonder and curiosity about the unknown. The visualization of sea monsters and other fantastical elements reflects the human proclivity to blend reality with imagination, serving a dual function: to captivate and to caution explorers venturing into new territories.

Moreover, the cultural significance embedded within the map's design speaks to the broader narrative surrounding the Age of Discovery. The symbols and legends employed were not simply arbitrary decorations; they contained cultural meanings and historical contexts that echoed the desires and fears of the people of the time. As cartography advanced as a discipline, symbols evolved to articulate increasingly complex geographic and political realities, informing not only navigators but also imperial ambitions that sought to assert dominance over newly encountered lands.

In conclusion, the Piri Reis Map is a remarkable artifact that exemplifies the intricate convergence of symbols, legends, and scales in the practice of cartography. Through the thoughtful embedding of navigational aids, cultural narratives, and artistic embellishments, Piri Reis crafted a work that not only guided explorers across uncharted waters but also invited them into a world rich with history, myth, and inquiry. The very fabric of the map expresses the essence of human curiosity, fostering a deeper understanding of our environment while acknowledging the myriad stories that traverse the landscapes it represents. As we continue to explore the layers contained within the Piri Reis Map, we are reminded of the profound impact of cartography on shaping perceptions, forging connections, and illuminating the complexities of the human experience in our pursuit of knowledge and adventure.

8.3. Geographical Myths and Realities

The Piri Reis Map is often celebrated for its intricate blend of myth and reality, captivating historians and explorers alike with its depiction of geographical features as well as its imaginative embellishments. This unique mix provides a rich ground for understanding how maps functioned not only as navigational tools but also as reflections of cultural beliefs and perceptions of the world during the early 16th century. To explore the geographical myths and realities encapsulated within the Piri Reis Map, one must first analyze the map's artistic interpretations alongside its empirical underpinnings.

At its core, the Piri Reis Map integrates a wealth of empirical data sourced from various navigational explorations while simultaneously stitching in rich mythological and allegorical elements that were prevalent in the imaginations of its time. The cartographic techniques applied in its creation underscore a commitment to rendering a world both known and unknown, where specific geographical features are drawn with notable accuracy, while other areas evoke fictional realms filled with speculation and legend. This dualistic nature reflects humanity's perennial quest to understand and represent its environment, highlighting the tension between factual observation and culturally infused interpretation.

For instance, the meticulous depiction of coastlines such as those of South America and the Caribbean indicates Piri Reis's access to firsthand observations, likely augmented by previous navigators' accounts. The accuracy with which certain prominent landmarks are rendered speaks to the scientific rigor of the mapmaking process. Yet, at the same time, embellishments—like mythical creatures that inhabit the oceanic expanses—remind viewers of the rich narratives that coalesced with exploratory endeavors. This encompassment invites reflection on how the human experience intertwines with geography, as people historically enriched their understanding of the world through the stories and the myths that traversed them.

The map's annotations serve an important function in contextualizing these geographical features and embellishments as well. Piri Reis carefully documented not only the coordinates of various territories but also the cultural narratives associated with them. The blend of indigenous descriptions alongside European perspectives creates a tapestry of knowledge that underscores the complexities of cultural exchange during a time marked by imperial expansion. Such representations prompt us to consider how history is constructed—not just from observations but also from interactions, negotiations, and often competing narratives.

Furthermore, it is essential to acknowledge how the Piri Reis Map contributes to a broader understanding of geographical knowledge, which was still developing amid the uncertainties of early modern exploration. As mythological representations filled gaps in knowledge, they reveal the limitations of contemporary understanding of geography. The map is a reflection of the time it was created, embodying a moment when exploration was driven by both empirical curiosity and the lure of the unknown. The presence of mythical lands and ambiguity around certain regions invites inquiry into the nature of maps as not only navigational instruments but also cultural artifacts that convey the aspirations and imaginations of their creators.

The geographical myths and realities illustrated through the Piri Reis Map serve to enrich our understanding of early modern cartographic practice and the enduring human endeavor to chart the contours of existence. They challenge us to critically examine the ways in which stories shaped perceptions of geography, demonstrating that maps are multifaceted representations grounded in both observation and interpretation. In this sense, the Piri Reis Map may not provide definitive truths about geographical territories, but rather potent insights into the human capacity to explore, imagine, and symbolize the vastness of the world around us.

This interplay between myth and reality in geographical representation continues to resonate, opening pathways for contemporary scholars to investigate the evolving narrative of cartography as a bridge between the factual and the fantastical. The Piri Reis Map stands as a compelling testament to the artistic and scientific endeavors of its time, merging the dual pursuits of understanding and wondering, and inviting us to reflect upon the intricacies of exploration that shape the very fabric of historical knowledge.

8.4. The Aesthetic Appeal of Maps

The aesthetic appeal of maps transcends mere utility; they encapsulate the intricacies of human thought and artistry. The Piri Reis Map, crafted in the early 16th century, exemplifies this relationship between form and function, acting as a vibrant reflection of its time, filled with artistic flourishes and intricate details that engage the viewer on various levels. As we delve into the aesthetic elements embedded within such cartographic works, we come to appreciate how they serve not only as navigational tools but also as vessels of culture, knowledge, and creativity.

First and foremost, one cannot overlook the visual harmony present in the Piri Reis Map. The careful balance of colors against parchment reflects a sophisticated understanding of the visual landscape. The use of vibrant blues for oceans and subtle browns and greens for land convey not just geographical realities but an artistic rendering that awakens an appreciation for the beauty of construction. The careful selection of colors involved functional implications as well; contrasting shades assist in distinguishing seas, coastlines, and territories, enabling navigators to process information at a glance, all the while maintaining an aesthetic appeal that engages the eye.

Beyond color, the cartographer's use of detailed illustrations enhances the map's artistic allure. Piri Reis painstakingly rendered the coastlines and significant landmarks, providing not merely outlines but depictions that evoke the textures and characteristics of the landscapes. The various embellishments—be it ships sailing on the waters, imaginative depictions of mythical sea creatures, or animals illustrated along coastal regions—bring the map to life, speaking to an artistic sensibility that deftly weaves together reality and imagination. Such representations engage viewers in a narrative of exploration, sparking curiosity and wonder about the myriad stories tied to different lands.

Moreover, the borders of the Piri Reis Map are ornate, visually framing the interior cartographic content and inviting exploration of the detailed narratives encapsulated within. These decorative elements serve a dual purpose: they not only enhance the aesthetic quality of the map but also establish a sense of cultural identity. The artistic motifs and patterns found in the map invoke the rich traditions of the Ottoman Empire, reflecting the cultural sophistication of the time. This desire to personalize functional documents mirrors broader artistic movements during the Renaissance when the interplay between aesthetics and utility became increasingly valued.

The intricate calligraphy on the map, with its elegantly crafted inscriptions, further contributes to its aesthetic appeal. Piri Reis's annotations convey essential navigational information and imbue the map with a scholarly gravitas, reflecting the intellectual pursuits of the age. The integration of clear yet beautifully styled scripts emphasizes the importance of communication in cartography, while simultaneously serving as a reminder of the artistry inherent in written language. Each inscription, crafted with care, invites viewers to not only examine geographical information but also to engage intellectually with the content presented.

Furthermore, the Piri Reis Map acts as a visual proposition of the interconnectedness of peoples and cultures during the Age of Discovery. The artistic embellishments and elaborate design elements suggest a broader narrative that speaks to the spirit of exploration, curiosity, and cultural exchange beyond mere mapping. Each aspect —be it color, imagery, or calligraphy—intertwines with the historical, cultural, and scientific practices of the time, creating a tapestry that narrates the complexities of geographic representation.

In conclusion, the aesthetic appeal of the Piri Reis Map transcends its primary function as a navigational tool by embodying the rich interplay between art and science. The map serves as a testament to the creative spirit of its time, engaging viewers through its vibrant colors, detailed illustrations, ornate borders, and elegant inscriptions. Understanding the intricacies of its design allows us to appreciate the broader implications of cartography as a cultural artifact—a means of communication that reflects both the technical advancements of the age and the enduring human narrative woven through exploration. As we engage with maps like the Piri Reis Map, we recognize that they represent not just territories but also the endless curiosity, creativity, and ambition that define the human journey.

8.5. Developments into the Modern Era

In the wake of the Age of Discovery, the Piri Reis Map emerged as a pivotal artifact that encapsulated both the cartographic advancements of the 16th century and the profound shifts in human understanding of the world. As explorers combed through territories previously shrouded in mystery, their experiences and observations significantly gained prominence in the cartographic representations of the time. The map created by Piri Reis stands as a testament to the evolving practices of mapping, marking the transition from medieval to early modern geographical interpretations.

In this modern era of cartography, the influence of the Piri Reis Map can be seen in multiple dimensions—each reflecting broader trends in geographic understanding and technological innovation. The historical context surrounding the creation of the map underscores the cultural syncretism that flourished during the Ottoman Empire, embodying the vital exchanges of knowledge across civilizations. Maps transitioned from mere representations of place to instruments of power that articulated empires' ambitions and aspirations, revealing the geopolitical landscape that shaped exploration.

One significant development in this modern cartographic evolution has been the introduction of advanced mapping technologies. The innovation of tools such as GPS, digital mapping applications, and satellite imagery has transformed how we perceive and engage with space. In this context, the Piri Reis Map serves as an important historical reference point, illustrating the antiquated methods of navigation contrasted against contemporary techniques that allow for unprecedented levels of accuracy and detail. The practices employed by Piri Reis and his contemporaries underscore the iterative nature of cartographic progress, where each generation builds upon the discoveries and methodologies of the past.

Furthermore, the Piri Reis Map's artistic elements propelled the recognition that maps are not solely functional artifacts but have the capacity to convey cultural narratives and social identities. As scholars and artists alike grapple with how maps influence perceptions of ownership and belonging, the layered storytelling woven into Piri Reis's work invigorates discussions on the cultural significance of cartography. This recognition of maps as cultural texts is vital in contemporary discourse, illustrating how geographical representations continue to shape our understanding of the world and mirror the dynamics of power.

In modern scholarship, the Piri Reis Map also invites ongoing reevaluation of historical narratives. The map's inclusion of speculative landmasses, indigenous knowledge, and diverse cultural influences raises critical questions about the nature of discovery and the construction of geographic knowledge. As researchers delve into the map's details, they are compelled to confront the complexities of cultural appropriation and representation amid the flourishing of empire-driven exploration. This dialogue enhances our comprehension of the conditions that shaped knowledge production about geography and encourages us to reconsider who has the authority to define and map the world.

The reactions and interpretations of the Piri Reis Map within academia highlight the multifaceted legacy it has left. Even as modern interpretations continue to emerge, the map stands as a powerful artifact that showcases the profound intersections of art, science, culture, and politics in the realm of cartography. It invites scholars and enthusiasts to engage with the historical contexts that gave rise to its creation while invoking contemporary conversations about the implications of mapping practices today.

The legacy of transformation catalyzed by the Piri Reis Map extends far beyond its physical representation on parchment. It embodies the ceaseless human curiosity to explore the unknown, a quest that has become increasingly significant as we confront the complexities of our globalized world. As we reflect on the developments into the modern era, the map inspires a deeper appreciation for the ongoing endeavors to chart the intricacies of Earth while reminding us of the spirit of inquiry that defines our collective journey as explorers of knowledge.

9. Encountering the Map: Reactions and Theories

9.1. Initial Reactions from Historians

The initial reactions from historians to the Piri Reis Map have been as varied as they are profound, reflecting a remarkable blend of fascination, skepticism, and analytical inquiry. When the map was rediscovered in 1929, it quickly ignited interest not only for its artistic and navigational merits but also for its implications regarding historical understanding. This early reaction, spurred by the rediscovery, laid the groundwork for subsequent scholarship and interpretations that would evolve significantly over the following decades.

Initially, historians were captivated by the sheer audacity of the Piri Reis Map. They marveled at Piri Reis's ability to depict the coastlines of regions like the Americas with notable accuracy at a time when such knowledge was thought to be scarce among Ottoman scholars. This perception was rooted in the broader context of the Age of Discovery, during which European powers were actively charting new territories. The map's intricate details and comprehensive coverage contributed to discussions around the extent of geographical knowledge accessible to the Ottomans and their engagement with contemporary navigational techniques.

Historians were particularly intrigued by the map's connections to existing cartographic traditions from Europe, the Islamic world, and indigenous knowledge. The blend of these diverse sources raised questions regarding cross-cultural exchange, prompting scholars to consider how navigational insights traveled across geographic and cultural borders. Early historians attempted to analyze the influences of Iberian explorations on Piri Reis's work, particularly in relation to the territories charted in South America, seeking to trace the lines of knowledge that culminated in his remarkable cartographic achievement.

However, initial reactions were not without a degree of skepticism. Some historians were cautious about ascribing too much historical significance to the map, questioning its reliability as a precise navigational tool. They argued that the map's speculative elements, including mythical features and uncertain landmasses, undermined its credibility as an accurate representation of geography. This line of thought underscored the complexities inherent in interpretation, where the intersection of observation, embellishment, and cultural narratives shaped the creation of maps in significant ways.

As discussions about the Piri Reis Map gained momentum, debates emerged surrounding Piri Reis's position as a cartographer within the Ottoman Empire. Some scholars lauded him as a pioneering figure in the blending of cultural influences, while others positioned him as part of a larger Ottoman naval tradition that was emblematic of imperial ambitions. This multifaceted view of Piri Reis's role resonated with historians who sought to contextualize his work within the broader narrative of the empire's efforts to assert dominance across maritime routes.

Moreover, the initial reactions also pointed to the potential implications of the Piri Reis Map for understanding historical narratives. Some historians began to consider how the existence of comprehensive maps like Piri Reis's challenged established views of geographic knowledge and exploration. This prompted a reevaluation of the traditional historical narratives that often centered European achievements while marginalizing contributions from non-European cultures. The Piri Reis Map arose as a symbol of this broader discourse, embodying the complexities of cultural exchange and the intersecting relationships between exploration, knowledge, and power.

Overall, the initial reactions from historians to the Piri Reis Map marked the inception of a dynamic field of inquiry that would continue to evolve over time. The map became a focal point for discussions about navigation, cross-cultural exchanges, and the very act of mapping—reflecting not only the technical prowess of Piri Reis but also the historical significance intertwined in his artistry. As scholars began to dissect the layers of meaning embedded within the map, a rich tapestry of interpretations emerged—each contributing to a multifaceted understanding of an artifact that continues to evoke curiosity and intrigue. The map's legacy thus became a living narrative, inspiring ongoing research and inquiry into the intersections of culture, history, and exploration, illuminating the enduring impact of Piri Reis's work far beyond its time.

9.2. Theories and Hypotheses

The exploration of theories and hypotheses surrounding the Piri Reis Map showcases the interplay of historical inquiry, cartographic analysis, and the quest for understanding that continues to influence contemporary scholarship. Since its rediscovery in 1929, this extraordinary artifact has generated a wealth of interpretations, each striving to unravel the complexities of its content, implications, and the societal and cultural context in which it was created. Within this dialogue, we encounter a variety of theories that address the map's anomalies, historical significance, and the very nature of knowledge production in the early 16th century.

One prominent theory revolves around the map's representation of regions like Antarctica, which was only confirmed to exist in the early 19th century. Some scholars hypothesize that the contours on the Piri Reis Map reflecting a southern landmass might indicate lost knowledge from ancient civilizations or earlier navigators that could have traversed those waters. This theory challenges the conventional timeline of discovery by suggesting that an understanding of Antarctica may have existed long before its official recognition—a notion that compels researchers to reconsider previous narratives about the limits of exploration and recording of geographical knowledge.

Another theory stems from scrutiny of the cartographic sources that Piri Reis relied upon to create his map. Historians contend that the Piri Reis Map amalgamates information from earlier medieval maps, European charts, and contributions from Arab geographers. This hypothesis highlights the possible connections between various cartographic traditions and emphasizes the importance of cultural exchange during the Age of Discovery. The map thus serves as a testament to the notion that knowledge production is inherently collaborative, transcending geographic and temporal boundaries.

Critics of the traditional Eurocentric view of exploration often argue that the significance of indigenous knowledge is underrepresented in the scholarly discourse surrounding the Piri Reis Map. A compelling line of inquiry posits that Piri Reis engaged actively with local knowledge systems as he navigated the Mediterranean and ventured into the Atlantic. The map's annotations, which contain references to local populations and their practices, support the hypothesis that indigenous insights informed Piri Reis's understanding of newly encountered lands. This perspective invites scholars to acknowledge the complexities of cartographic practices and to consider the multifaceted dialogues that occurred in the formation of geographical knowledge.

Furthermore, theories examining the artistic elements of the Piri Reis Map highlight the role of myth and allegory within cartography. Scholars explore how the aesthetics of the map intertwine with geographic representation to create a narrative that tells stories of exploration, cultures, and the unknown. The inclusion of mythical creatures and imaginative landscapes raises questions about the motivations behind such embellishments. One hypothesis is that these artistic choices served not only decorative purposes but also acted as cautionary symbols, invoking the mystique and dangers of uncharted waters. By marrying art to geographic detail, Piri Reis contributed to a narrative that mirrors the human desire to comprehend and interpret the world.

Finally, thematic theories addressing the ideological dimensions of the Piri Reis Map argue that it encapsulates the spirit of Ottoman imperial ambitions during a time of expansion and cultural renaissance. The incorporation of detailed geographical knowledge alongside grandiose representations of the empire's reach indicates an effort to assert power and dominance over maritime routes. This hypothesis emphasizes how maps function not only as tools of navigation but also as instruments of political expression, reflecting the aspirations and identity of the empires that produced them.

In conclusion, the myriad theories and hypotheses surrounding the Piri Reis Map illuminate the complexities and nuances of understanding this remarkable artifact. They reflect a broader cultural discourse that seeks to reconcile old and new geographies while probing into the nature of knowledge production and representation. As scholars continue to explore and debate these interpretations, the Piri Reis Map remains a dynamic testament to the enduring inquiries that define cartography's legacy—a legacy that continues to shape our understanding and appreciation of historical exploration, cultural exchange, and the intricacies of mapping the world.

9.3. Modern Interpretations

Modern interpretations of the Piri Reis Map encapsulate a diverse array of perspectives that seek to unpack the significance of this extraordinary artifact in the broader tapestry of history, exploration, and cartography. The map, created in 1513 by the Ottoman admiral and cartographer Piri Reis, has become a focal point for scholars, historians, and enthusiasts alike. Its intricate details and layered narratives prompt not only appreciation for its artistic and technical achievements but also deeper inquiries into the socio-political and cultural implications that permeate the Age of Discovery.

Contemporary analyses often emphasize the cross-cultural influences present in the map, highlighting how Piri Reis synthesized knowledge from various sources, including earlier European maps, Arabic texts, and indigenous accounts. This recognition of the map as a product of intercultural dialogue underscores the importance of acknowledging diverse contributions to the construction of geographical knowledge. Modern interpretations encourage viewers to move beyond a Eurocentric lens and appreciate the richness of the exchanges that occurred during the time of exploration, reflecting a more nuanced understanding of the global history of maps.

Moreover, studies of the Piri Reis Map increasingly focus on its role as an artifact that bridges the worlds of art and science. Scholars note how the map encapsulates the dynamic interplay between navigational precision and artistic expression. The vibrant colors, elaborate illustrations, and embellished borders speak to a Renaissance ethos that valued both empirical knowledge and aesthetic beauty. This melding of art and science is seen as indicative of a transformative shift in how societies perceived and represented geography, influencing subsequent cartographic practices in both Ottoman and European contexts.

In addition to its artistic and cultural significance, modern interpretations also delve into the map's implications for understanding the mysteries of uncharted territories. The Piri Reis Map has ignited debates over the accuracy of early cartographers' depictions of the Americas and other regions, with scholars examining the map's speculative elements. The presence of imaginary landmasses and mythical creatures in the map has led some to question the beliefs and practices of the explorers who populated these maps with fantastical narratives. Modern interpretations underscore how these mythical components act as windows into the psyche of explorers who navigated the unknown, exposing the tensions inherent in their quests for knowledge.

Another thread in contemporary scholarship examines the Piri Reis Map as a provocation to established historical narratives. By detailing territories previously thought to remain unexplored by the Ottoman Empire during Europe's Age of Discovery, it invites historians to re-evaluate the complexities of mapping practices and the geopolitical motivations behind them. This recontextualization challenges the traditional portrayal of the Ottomans merely as conservative custodians of knowledge, arguing instead that they were engaged in a vibrant exchange of ideas and navigational practices that shaped the world's collective understanding.

The thematic examinations revolving around the Piri Reis Map reveal a dynamic intersection of historical inquiry, cartographic evolution, and cultural discourse. Contemporary interpretations resound with the call for a continuous reassessment of historical artifacts—recognizing that the narratives constructed around these works can significantly evolve in light of new knowledge and perspectives.

In summary, modern interpretations of the Piri Reis Map foster a greater appreciation for its complexity, reflecting the richness of cultural exchanges and the shifting paradigms that define how we understand exploration and geography. As scholarship continues to unfold, the legacy of the Piri Reis Map challenges conventional boundaries and illuminates the multifaceted nature of maps as cultural documents. They embody narratives that transcend their surfaces and invite us to actively engage with the histories they represent, prompting new inquiries into the world of exploration, discovery, and the imagination.

9.4. Challenges to Established History

The Piri Reis Map, with its vivid blend of myth and empirical observation, poses significant challenges to established historical narratives about exploration, cartography, and cultural exchanges of the early modern world. As a pioneering document from the early 16th century, the map reflects a moment of transformation in geographical understanding, and its nuances compel scholars to reconsider long-held beliefs about navigation, knowledge production, and the interconnectedness of different cultures during the Age of Discovery.

At first glance, the Piri Reis Map challenges the conventional wisdom that portrays the Ottoman Empire as dormant in the shadow of European powers during the Age of Exploration. Instead, Piri Reis emerges as a figure who synthesized diverse knowledge from various cultures—European maritime charts, Islamic navigational practices, and indigenous accounts—with remarkable skill. This synthesis unveils the existence of a rich, transnational exchange of ideas that complicates the narrative of geographical advancement being firmly in the hands of European explorers alone. The elements embedded within the map offer a glimpse of an Ottoman perspective that was keenly aware of wider geographic realities and engaged actively with contemporaneous explorations.

Moreover, the map's depiction of lands that had only recently been charted by European explorers, alongside its inclusion of speculative features, leads to questions about the integrity and reliability of historical accounts regarding the "discovery" of new territories. Some interpretations suggest that the Piri Reis Map incorporates knowledge that may predate the colonial ventures that are often highlighted in European narratives, suggesting that there existed a fluid intermingling of geographical information acquired through diverse means —trade, exploration, and cultural exchange—that wasn't limited to an imperialistic framework.

The Piri Reis Map also promotes discussions regarding the representation of indigenous peoples. The annotations accompanying various regions frequently reference local populations and their customs, hinting at a level of engagement that counterbalances the predominant narrative wherein indigenous voices are largely silenced or overlooked. By offering insight into how European explorers, including those from the Ottoman Empire, documented and interacted with indigenous cultures, the map enables a reevaluation of the historical dynamics at play during European colonial expansion.

As such, the Piri Reis Map becomes a catalyst for critical inquiry, as modern scholars increasingly recognize the importance of analyzing historical artifacts through multiple lenses. The map's existence not only invites a reassessment of the dynamics of power and knowledge propagation across cultures but also fosters conversations about the ethical implications surrounding representation and the narratives that shape our understanding of past encounters.

The Piri Reis Map thus stands as an emblematic challenge to established historical narratives. It invites scholars and enthusiasts alike to reconsider the complexities of exploration, the fluidity of knowledge production, and the interactions between cultures that defined both the old and the new geographies of the world. As researchers delve deeper into the layers of meaning within this remarkable artifact, they inevitably confront the questions of how history is constructed and the narratives we choose to embrace in narrating the past.

In advocating for ongoing examination and re-evaluation of historical artifacts like the Piri Reis Map, we underscore the importance of understanding history as a living dialogue—constantly evolving and shaped by fresh assessments and interpretations. The intricacies encapsulated within the Piri Reis Map serve as a reminder that history is not a static narrative; rather, it is an ever-present conversation that necessitates vigilance in our quest for deeper understanding and appreciation of the world's cultural legacies.

9.5. The Importance of Re-evaluation

The tradition of re-evaluation in the context of historical artifacts, especially in the field of cartography, plays an essential role in shaping our understanding of the past. The Piri Reis Map, created in 1513, serves not merely as a navigational tool but as a vital cultural and historical artifact that requires scrutiny across varied dimensions. The act of re-evaluation is critical; it encourages historians and scholars to scrutinize established narratives, explore new methodologies, and integrate fresh perspectives into the discourse surrounding this remarkable creation.

The call for continued assessment arises from the intricacies embedded within the Piri Reis Map itself. Upon its rediscovery in 1929, historians initially perceived it primarily as an emblem of the Ottoman Empire's navigational capabilities during the Age of Exploration. Nevertheless, within its rich symbolism and layered narratives lie multiple interpretations that challenge initial readings. An in-depth examination of the map uncovers a wealth of information—details about socio-political interactions, the dissemination of knowledge across cultures, and the complexities of imperial ambitions—which reflect broader historical themes. Such insights reinforce the necessity of re-evaluation to enhance our understanding of cartographic practices that once thrived in an interconnected world.

Furthermore, historical maps like the Piri Reis Map serve as a window into the changing perceptions of geography over time. The map's incorporation of accounts from diverse navigational traditions illustrates a fundamental truth: knowledge is a fluid entity that evolves as cultures interact. By continuously re-examining the map, scholars can unveil the depths of cross-cultural dialogues that shaped understandings of geography within an era marked by exploration and curiosity. This re-evaluation compels us to reconsider assumptions rooted in Eurocentric narratives, elevating the voices and contributions of non-European societies that significantly informed the map.

The significance of the Piri Reis Map extends beyond purely scholarly pursuits; it serves as a testament to the ongoing relevance of cartographic practices in contemporary dialogue around culture and history. As discussions about representation, identity, and power dynamics emerge in the modern context, the map becomes an engaging artifact that invites re-evaluation through contemporary frameworks. It provides an arena for debates over the ethics of mapping, cultural appropriation, and the need for inclusive narratives that honor the myriad voices that contribute to our collective understanding of geography.

The value of re-evaluation reaches into educational contexts as well, as educators seek to instill a critical framework for analyzing historical artifacts among students. Engaging with maps like the Piri Reis Map in educational settings fosters a spirit of inquiry, inviting learners to explore how maps function as cultural documents and pathways for understanding diverse historical narratives. The importance of approaching such artifacts with a discerning mind cannot be overstated, as it encourages learners to navigate the complexities of historical interpretation while fostering an appreciation for collaboration across cultures.

In conclusion, the importance of re-evaluation in relation to the Piri Reis Map emerges as a vital endeavor that spans scholarly, educational, and cultural realms. It facilitates a deeper understanding of the interconnected heritage shaped by exploration and mapping while acknowledging the ongoing evolution of knowledge through cultural exchange. As we engage with this remarkable artifact, we embark on a journey that transcends its historical boundaries and invites us to reflect critically on the legacies of exploration, representation, and knowledge that continue to resonate today. In doing so, we honor not only Piri Reis's contributions but also the enduring human quest for understanding the world—an endeavor grounded in curiosity, reflection, and collaboration that bridges the past and present.

10. The Legacy of Piri Reis

10.1. A Lasting Influence on Cartography

The influence of Piri Reis on the field of cartography resonates far beyond the pages of history, crafting a legacy that continues to shape the practices and philosophies associated with map-making today. His exceptional work not only embodies the spirit of exploration during the Age of Discovery but also integrates diverse strands of geographical knowledge that underscore the interconnected nature of various cultures. As we delve into the lasting impact of Piri Reis, we see how his methodologies, artistic designs, and sinuous narratives have left an indelible mark on cartography.

The Piri Reis Map is a confluence of scientific exploration and artistic creativity, a hallmark of a transformative period in map-making. One of the most significant contributions of Piri Reis was his ability to synthesize knowledge from multiple sources—European nautical charts, Arabian texts, and local indigenous Knowledge. This approach not only showcased an advanced understanding of geography but also called attention to the necessity of cross-cultural exchange in the production of accurate maps. By incorporating diverse perspectives, Piri Reis elevated the potential of cartography as a means of enriching collective geographic understanding.

In the wake of Piri Reis's remarkable synthesis of information, future cartographers began to embrace this interdisciplinary approach. The acknowledgment that maps could serve as documents of cultural narrative propelled an evolution in the philosophy of mapping. Subsequent map-makers followed in Piri Reis's footsteps by incorporating local knowledge and perspectives, and integrating artistic designs that conveyed engaging stories about the landscapes they depicted. This shift laid the groundwork for a more holistic understanding of geography—one that emphasized the intersections between empirical observation and the rich tapestry of human experiences.

Piri Reis's artistic embellishments further solidified his influence on cartographic practices. The vibrant colors and intricate decorations found within his map not only provided visual appeal but also became templates for conveying cultural narratives. In blending aesthetics with functionality, Piri Reis challenged later cartographers to merge artistic expression with scientific rigor. Maps evolved into reflections of cultural identity, capturing both geographic details and the narratives of people and places, transforming cartography into an art form that resonated with the viewers on multiple levels.

Moreover, the Piri Reis Map has sparked ongoing scholarly interest, leading to the examination of its historical context and cartographic techniques. Researchers have delved into the intricacies of the map, analyzing its representation of coastlines, symbols, and geographic anomalies. Such studies have illuminated the influence of Piri Reis on future generations of map-makers, prompting a reevaluation of his contributions and their significance in the broader narrative of cartographic history.

Piri Reis's legacy is also witnessed in the way contemporary historians and cartographers approach mapping practices today. His willingness to draw from a vast array of sources and to embrace ambiguity in navigation laid precedence for inclusive mapping methodologies that prioritize collaboration and cultural exchange. Modern cartographic practices increasingly honor the wisdom of indigenous knowledge systems while cultivating a deeper understanding of the interconnections between geography and culture.

In conclusion, the lasting influence of Piri Reis on cartography is palpable within the evolving methodologies, artistic philosophies, and cultural narratives sustained through mapping practices. The Piri Reis Map endures as a beacon of the human dimension of exploration, ultimately showing that cartography transcends mere geographic representation. As we navigate the complexities of the contemporary world, the legacy of Piri Reis—a testament to the beauty of interdisciplinary inquiry—continues to inspire future generations of map-makers to celebrate the rich tapestry of knowledge and human endeavor that defines our understanding of geography and exploration.

10.2. Roles and Perceptions Over Time

The Piri Reis Map stands as a testament to the interplay between exploration and the evolving perceptions of cartographers, particularly Piri Reis himself, across different eras. The map's journey from an Ottoman navigational tool to a global historical artifact illustrates the shifting roles attributed to its creator and the broader implications of his work within various cultural, political, and scholarly contexts.

Initially, Piri Reis was perceived primarily as a skilled cartographer and navigator within the Ottoman Empire. His contribution to maritime navigation was recognized, particularly through the production of "Kitab-ı Bahriye" (Book of Navigation), which provided detailed information on the Mediterranean coasts. The Piri Reis Map, created in 1513, not only served as a practical navigational aid but showcased the Empire's intellectual prowess during a time of significant expansion. His reputation was closely tied to the Ottoman naval forces, and he played a crucial role in asserting naval dominance in the Mediterranean.

However, as the map fell into obscurity following the decline of the empire, perceptions of Piri Reis became layered and complex. Rediscovered in the early 20th century, the map catalyzed discussions among historians and geographers about its implications for understanding the Age of Exploration. Piri Reis's reputation transformed from a regional figure to one of international significance, as scholars began to appreciate the nuances of his work, recognizing him not merely as an Ottoman cartographer but as a pivotal figure whose contributions bridged cultures and knowledge systems.

Modern perceptions of Piri Reis extend beyond the confines of geographic mapping. The map has become emblematic of the complexities of cultural exchange during the Age of Discovery, prompting discussions on the intersections of imperial ambition, artistic expression, and the narratives that enriched cartographic practices. Piri Reis's incorporation of diverse sources—from indigenous knowledge to European maritime charts—has elevated his status as a symbol of intellectual collaboration across cultures.

Moreover, contemporary scholars examine Piri Reis's role through the lens of intersectionality and post-colonial perspectives. His mapping practices are viewed as a focal point for discussing the implications of European expansionism and the resulting shifts in power dynamics. The map becomes a vehicle for engaging with critical inquiries around representation, knowledge production, and the ethical dimensions of cartography in a globalized world. This reevaluation challenges the traditional narratives of discovery and conquest, highlighting the complexities inherent in cultural interactions.

The legacy of Piri Reis has also found resonance in popular culture, where he is frequently referenced in literature, documentaries, and educational materials. These portrayals reflect the enduring fascination with exploration and the mysteries of early cartography. The Piri Reis Map often features in discussions around the historical context of navigation, serving as an entry point to explore the broader themes of cultural exchange and the human spirit of inquiry. This representation helps to cement his place in popular consciousness as a figure of significance, akin to other well-known explorers.

In the academic sphere, ongoing research continues to spotlight Piri Reis and his contributions to cartography. Scholars explore various aspects of his work—be it his navigational techniques, artistic elements, or the socio-political implications of his maps. This modern scholarly focus encompasses interdisciplinary approaches, connecting insights from history, geography, art history, and cultural studies to enrich our understanding of his contributions.

Lastly, as the Piri Reis Map garners renewed attention, preserving it becomes crucial for future generations. The map is not only an artifact of immense historical value but also a symbol of the complexities of exploration and cross-cultural exchange. Efforts to conserve and maintain the map within museums and archives speak to the recognition of its importance in narratives of history, heritage, and identity.

In conclusion, the roles and perceptions of Piri Reis have evolved significantly over time, reflecting broader societal shifts and an ever-deepening understanding of cartography and exploration. The Piri Reis Map remains a compelling artifact that encapsulates the intersection of knowledge, culture, and human curiosity—prompting ongoing inquiry, appreciation, and engagement with the intricate legacies of the past.

10.3. Piri Reis in Popular Culture

The enduring influence of Piri Reis is not limited to historical discourse; it has permeated various facets of popular culture, literature, and education, illustrating the mapmaker's significance in contemporary dialogues about exploration and cultural exchange. The Piri Reis Map, an artifact of the early 16th century, remains a point of fascination, prompting reflections on the complexities of navigation, cartography, and the human spirit of inquiry that defines our understanding of geography.

In literature, references to Piri Reis often evoke themes of adventure, discovery, and mystery. His name surfaces in novels that explore historical fiction or narratives about exploration, where authors leverage the intrigue surrounding the Piri Reis Map to dramatize the quests of explorers and adventurers. Literature frequently portrays him as a symbol of the spirit of inquiry that characterized the Age of Discovery, framing him within adventurous narratives that celebrate the pursuit of knowledge and the unknown.

Media representations of the Piri Reis Map have further extended its reach into popular culture. Documentaries and educational programs delve into the life and work of Piri Reis, using visual storytelling to highlight his contributions within a broader historical context. These productions often feature the Piri Reis Map as a central artifact, illuminating the artistry and technical skill behind its creation while also emphasizing the cultural dialogues that were essential during the period of exploration. The combination of historical analysis and compelling visuals effectively engages contemporary audiences in the continued relevance of Piri Reis's work.

In the realm of education, the Piri Reis Map frequently finds its place within curricula that focus on world history, geography, and art. Educators utilize the map to illustrate not only the technical aspects of cartography but also the cultural narratives entwined within it. Students are encouraged to analyze the intersections of different cultures, knowledge systems, and artistic expressions encapsulated in the map. This educational engagement fosters critical thinking about how maps shape our understanding of identity, territory, and the shared human experience.

Furthermore, the Piri Reis Map's enduring presence in popular discourse has led to increased interest in its historical significance among new generations. Conferences, research initiatives, and online platforms dedicated to exploring historical explorations often spotlight Piri Reis, facilitating discussions that weave together historical narratives and contemporary interpretations of exploration. This sustained engagement underscores the potential for interdisciplinary collaboration to enrich our understanding of Piri Reis's contributions and the impact of mapping practices throughout history.

The preservation of the Piri Reis Map itself presents both opportunities and challenges, as its status as a national treasure demands sustained efforts to safeguard this invaluable artifact for future generations. The map is housed in the Topkapi Palace Museum in Istanbul, where it has sat since its rediscovery. Preservation efforts focus on protecting the map from environmental degradation, ensuring that future scholars and enthusiasts can continue to engage with it. Conservation projects involve meticulously controlling temperature and humidity levels in the display area to minimize potential damage to the parchment and ink.

Moreover, digital technologies have emerged as crucial tools in the preservation of the Piri Reis Map. Digitization initiatives enable the creation of high-resolution images that can be disseminated widely, allowing scholars and the public alike to access the map for research and educational purposes. This emphasis on digital preservation not only enhances accessibility but also serves to engage a broader audience in the study of cartography, geography, and history.

Challenges persist in balancing public access to the map while safeguarding its integrity as a fragile historical document. The imperative to present the Piri Reis Map in a way that engages contemporary audiences must also contend with the need for careful conservation practices. Awareness campaigns about the importance of safeguarding cultural heritage support efforts to generate funding and resources for preservation projects, ultimately ensuring that future generations may appreciate and learn from Piri Reis's legacy.

In conclusion, Piri Reis's impact and the legacy of the Piri Reis Map extend beyond the confines of history and academia, unfolding within popular culture, literature, and education. The map serves as a powerful artifact that invites ongoing exploration and inquiry, spurring discourse that centers on exploration, navigation, and cultural identity. As preservation efforts continue to safeguard this remarkable piece of history, its role in shaping modern interpretations of cartography and geographic narrative serves as a testament to humanity's ceaseless curiosity and quest for understanding our world. Piri Reis's journey—from an Ottoman cartographer to a symbol of exploration—continues to inspire new generations and enrich our collective understanding of geographical heritage.

10.4. Modern Scholarly Work

Modern scholarly work surrounding the Piri Reis Map reflects a dynamic interplay between historical analysis, advances in cartographic science, and interdisciplinary approaches to understanding the map's significance in both its contemporary context and in our present day. Scholars, historians, and geographers have devoted considerable effort to unraveling the intricacies of the map, its creator, and its implications for the broader narrative of exploration and cultural exchange. This scholarly engagement not only honors the legacy of Piri Reis but also contributes to an ongoing dialogue about the roles, practices, and evolution of cartography.

Recent work has sought to place the Piri Reis Map within the larger landscape of early modern cartography, emphasizing its value as both a navigational tool and a cultural artifact. Researchers have increasingly recognized that maps of this era are not just technical documents; they embody a confluence of knowledge, artistry, and cultural perceptions that define the societies that produced them. The multidisciplinary nature of modern scholarly efforts means that scholars from history, geography, art history, and cultural studies are all contributing insights, enriching the understanding of the map beyond its initial context.

One significant avenue of research focuses on the map's synthesis of knowledge from diverse sources. Scholars have analyzed the interplay between European cartographic traditions, Arabic navigational texts, and indigenous knowledge that Piri Reis incorporated into his work. This cross-cultural examination highlights the collaborative nature of knowledge production; it invites inquiries into how cartographic practices birthed from various cultural legacies contributed to broader understandings of geographical spaces during the Age of Exploration. By engaging with this discourse, modern scholars challenge the notion of a singular narrative of discovery, revealing instead a web of interactions that inclusive interpretations.

Additionally, contemporary scholars have explored Piri Reis's use of artistic and mythical elements as a means of attracting attention and conveying messages about maritime exploration. The balance between empirical observation and artistic embellishment in his map reflects the cultural values and beliefs of the time. Recent studies emphasize how such representations invite deeper reflections on the human experience of exploration, cultural encounters, and the representation of the unknown. This approach speaks to a growing recognition among scholars that maps serve not only navigational purposes but also communicate the hopes, fears, and aspirations of their creators.

Modern technology has also transformed the methodologies employed in researching the Piri Reis Map. Digital cartography, GIS

(Geographic Information Systems), and sophisticated imaging techniques enable researchers to analyze the map's features and its underlying data in unprecedented detail. Scholars can now engage in spatial analyses, allowing for discernible patterns and insights that were previously obscured. Through digital projects, the map can be examined alongside other historical documents, manuscripts, and artifacts, enhancing intertextual analyses and broadening the scope of inquiry.

Moreover, the practice of involving a diverse array of scholarly perspectives has garnered increased attention, emphasizing the importance of inclusive narratives in historical research. Scholars are increasingly examining how indigenous knowledge and interactions with local populations are recorded within the map, challenging traditional narratives that prioritize European perspectives. This inclusive approach promotes a more nuanced understanding of the cultural exchanges that define the Age of Discovery and invites further exploration of the implications for contemporary discussions around representation and power dynamics.

Finally, the Piri Reis Map continues to be a focal point of conferences, workshops, and academic publications, demonstrating its significance in both historical and modern contexts. The scholarly work devoted to the Piri Reis Map not only enriches our understanding of this remarkable artifact but also contributes to broader conversations about cartography, exploration, and cultural exchange. In engaging with the richness of its complexities, researchers are paving the way for ongoing inquiries, helping to ensure that the legacy of Piri Reis, his map, and the spirit of exploration it embodies remains vibrant and relevant for future generations.

As the dialogue surrounding the Piri Reis Map expands within academic circles and beyond, it illuminates the multifaceted nature of cartography—a discipline that continues to evolve, drawing from the past while shaping contemporary understandings of the world. Modern scholarly work devoted to Piri Reis serves as an embodiment of this living legacy, reflecting humanity's enduring quest for knowledge and understanding of our ever-changing environment.

10.5. Preservation of the Map

The preservation of the Piri Reis Map is a critical endeavor that underscores the importance of safeguarding cultural heritage for future generations. As a remarkable artifact of cartography from the early 16th century, the map has historical, artistic, and scientific significance, capturing the essence of an era marked by exploration, cultural exchange, and the evolution of geographical knowledge. However, the fragility of the materials and the passage of time present formidable challenges that necessitate diligent conservation efforts.

The map is crafted on parchment, a material historically chosen for its durability compared to paper, yet it remains susceptible to environmental factors such as humidity, temperature fluctuations, and light exposure. The parchment used for the Piri Reis Map, an animal hide, can undergo changes over time, leading to brittleness, discoloration, and potential degradation. Conservationists must carefully monitor these conditions to ensure that the map remains stable and free from deterioration.

To combat the threats posed by environmental conditions, preservation efforts involve maintaining a controlled environment tailored to the specific needs of the map. This includes regulating temperature and humidity levels within the display area and utilizing UV-filtering glass in frames to shield it from harmful light exposure. Such measures are essential to prolonging the life of the map, ensuring that its intricate details and vibrant colors remain visible for scholars and the public to engage with.

Additionally, conservationists use specialized techniques to assess the current condition of the map and develop appropriate restoration strategies. Non-invasive imaging technologies can reveal hidden details, layers, and structural issues without directly affecting the artifact itself. This advanced assessment allows conservators to create a comprehensive plan, addressing issues like tears, creases, and any signs of fading colors that may have occurred over time.

In preserving the Piri Reis Map, there is also a strong focus on documentation. Thorough records of the map's condition, conservation treatments, and environmental data are maintained as part of a comprehensive conservation strategy. This documentation not only enhances awareness about the map's history but also informs future conservation work, providing a foundation for ongoing research while fostering transparency and accountability within preservation practices.

The importance of public outreach and education cannot be overstated in the preservation of the Piri Reis Map. Engaging the public through exhibitions, educational programs, and digital initiatives creates greater awareness about the significance of preserving cultural artifacts. This outreach fosters a sense of shared responsibility for safeguarding historical treasures, promoting empathy and understanding around the map's cultural and historical narratives.

In the age of technology, digital preservation has emerged as a vital tool in the conservation of historical maps like that of Piri Reis. Creating high-resolution digital versions allows for widespread access to the map's intricacies while minimizing the need for physical handling. Digitalization enables scholars, educators, and the public to explore the contents of the map and engage in analyses that would otherwise risk damaging the original artifact. This approach extends the map's legacies into the digital realm, ensuring that its knowledge and stories remain accessible even beyond the limitations of physical preservation.

Moreover, collaboration among institutions is essential in fostering preservation efforts. Partnerships between museums, universities, and cultural heritage organizations can lead to the sharing of resources, expertise, and best practices. Such collaborations can significantly enhance conservation initiatives, ensuring that knowledge about preservation methods is disseminated widely and fostering a collective effort in safeguarding cultural heritage.

In conclusion, the preservation of the Piri Reis Map is a multifaceted commitment that highlights the necessity of protecting historical artifacts not just as objects of study, but as living testimonies to our shared heritage. The combination of environmental control, advanced conservation techniques, thorough documentation, public engagement, digital initiatives, and collaborative efforts significantly contributes to the map's longevity. Preservation serves as both a responsibility and an opportunity—a chance to honor the legacy of Piri Reis while ensuring that future generations can continue to explore the intricate narratives and cultural legacies embedded within this remarkable artifact of cartography. The Piri Reis Map, as a symbol of exploration and knowledge exchange, deserves the unwavering dedication required for its preservation, embodying the spirit of humanity's ceaseless quest to chart and understand our shared world.

Made in United States
Orlando, FL
28 January 2025